WITHDRAWN

*Manager Today,
Executive Tomorrow*

Manager Today,
Executive Tomorrow

Charles C. Vance
DIRECTOR OF CORPORATE COMMUNICATIONS
JOSLYN MFG. AND SUPPLY CO.
CHICAGO, ILLINOIS

ROBERT E. KRIEGER PUBLISHING COMPANY
MALABAR, FLORIDA
1983

658.409
V277m

Original Edition   1974
Reprint Edition   1983

Printed and Published by
ROBERT E. KRIEGER PUBLISHING COMPANY, INC.
KRIEGER DRIVE
MALABAR, FLORIDA 32950

Copyright © 1974 by McGraw-Hill, Inc.
Reprinted by Arrangement

All rights reserved. No part of this book may be reproduced in any form or by any electronic or mechanical means including information storage and retrieval systems without permission in writing from the publisher. All requests for permission to reproduce material from this work should be directed to the McGraw-Hill Book Company.

Printed in the United States of America

Library of Congress Cataloging in Publication Data

Vance, Charles C.
  Manager today, executive tomorrow.

  Reprint. Originally published: New York : McGraw-Hill, 1974.
  Includes index.
  1. Executive ability. 2. Psychology, Industrial.
I. Title.
[HF5500.2.V33 1983]   658.4'09   82-14865
ISBN 0-89874-554-3

Contents

Preface ix

ONE ***The Psychology of Measuring the Impact of Others in Your World*** *1*

Realistic attitudes about others. What others want from you. The "fits" and the "misfits." The "we-were-here-ahead-of-you" people. The ones with the competitive neurosis. Unavoidable conflicts. Being aware of dangers created by others. Why you must write off some people. True friends. Complications of the business world and their effect on your life-style. Turning the impact of others into an upward force for you.

TWO ***The Psychology of Knowing Yourself Better*** *27*

So you think you know who you are? Early start of our problems. The "because-it's-me" attitude. Getting a clear look at yourself. The grip of emotions. Using emotions that help. Handling tension and anxiety. Checklist of good and bad emotions. Cutting those "puppet strings." Proving the world doesn't revolve around you. How you look to your family. Why you do what you do. Your aggression level. Knowing your affinity for leadership. What have you done to help yourself? Deciding where you need improvement.

THREE ***Why No One Can Keep You from the Top . . . but You*** *55*

Examining your dissatisfaction. The type of people who are at the top. What those at the top want from you. What those at the top will give you. How you measure up to top-management requirements. Understanding the concept of the corporation. Looking at the changes taking place in United States business. Where you will fit at the top.

FOUR Your Master Plan for Getting Yourself Going 76

Starting your personal master plan. Using the go-ahead power within you. Selecting opportunities for gaining attention. Perfecting the art of being organized. Strengthening your organization — for your benefit. Building your ability to handle trouble. Doing what you can to step up productivity. Using this yardstick to measure your own maturity. Checking out the men who are ahead of you. Making a work list of rules for your daily conduct. Checking yourself out for "emotional common sense." Grappling with the large-corporation problems. Editing your master plan for getting yourself going.

FIVE Removing the No. 1 Stumbling Block—Human Conflict 99

Understanding the WHY of human conflict. Why most people haven't used their full potential. Emotions that cause people to "hang-fire" in their business lives. Understanding your subordinates' hidden emotions. Dealing with subordinates and their emotions. Keeping yourself from creating conflicts. The tragic side of human conflict in business. Sensing the "why" of what is going on in a person's mind.

SIX Moving Along by Mastering Others 121

Inward information. Outward information. Goal setting. You're the example. The advantages of listening. Mistakes and how they help you move ahead with your subordinates. Training your subordinates in better work habits. Effecting change. Emphasizing enterprise. The self-help thrust. Making committees work. Promoting the successful subordinates. Getting rid of the human failures.

SEVEN Picking Up Speed by Polishing Your Executive Skills 139

The broad background of the good executive. Why adding new skills is essential. You are always a salesperson, you are a purchasing agent, a marketing manager, a manager of time, a manager of profits, a financial manager, a forecasting manager, a recruitment manager, a manager of meetings, a manager of communications, a manager of authority, a manager of accountability.

EIGHT **Zooming Along by Tying It All Together ... Firmly 158**

What is really important to you? Clearing away the cobwebs of short vision. Management hurdles. Management can be beautiful. Coping with competitive peers. Dealing with the stereotypes. Meeting new people successfully. Handling misfits and trouble makers. The shortage of well-rounded executives. Helping yourself with public speaking. Are you aiming high enough?

NINE **Evaluating Your Progress at Checkpoints Alpha, Baker, and Charlie 177**

A preliminary check on your basic attitudes. You're the boss of yourself. What we mean by "goals." Understanding your boss. How much are you helping the corporation? What are you doing to become more effective?

TEN **Why the Lessons of Today Will Make You the Leader of Tomorrow 197**

Ten reasons why people fail. Ten reasons why people succeed. Ten reasons why you can make it. What to do tomorrow, next month, next year, in moving upward. How's your view of the top now? The "magic thoughts" that keep you refreshed. Go ahead, press the ignition button!

Index 221

Preface

One of the great truths of the business world, one that you must learn for yourself, is that you can move yourself smoothly from a manager's position to an executive position. This book was written to help you rise more swiftly and more directly to where you want to go in the organization.

Organizations don't move individuals to the top. Individuals move themselves to the top. The organization is merely the *structure* by which those who make the most effort and who are the most flexible can develop from managers into executives.

In this book you will see that you can make it to the top. Chapter by chapter, you will see that a more clear understanding of the psychology of leadership on your part will give you a more forceful control over your emotions and will enable you to manage yourself far more productively, to work more smoothly with other people to accomplish objectives, and to learn not to try for something over your head until you are well equipped to handle the larger task.

You will see that as a manager on your way up to becoming an executive you actually are a leader in development. Leadership is one of the most valuable commodities in the business world. It is what makes the difference between your being a winner or a loser.

No one is blocking your way to the executive position on which you have your sights set. This book will show you how you avoid setting up obstacles for yourself, how to seize every opportunity to advance yourself, and how to develop your own leadership style that will carry you past problems that could easily sidetrack you or delay your rise to the top.

Some managers, I have observed, are torn emotionally because they never learned how to use their manager psychology to achieve a position of real leadership. It is leadership that wins the satisfying executive's title and the other advantages of success.

Many managers seem to be in a near-desperate search for "nuts-and-bolts" advice on how to win success in the business world while they overlook the most essential leadership ingredients of success. To repeat, these ingredients are the ability to live effectively with oneself, to manage other people productively, and to prepare oneself ceaselessly to work beyond one's present capability.

Like some of these people, you perhaps have discovered that in today's fast-paced business world you are trapped between what you are and what you would like to be. Like them, perhaps you have an uneasy desire to find the "right way" to live your life and to find "the right key" to open the door to the executive office you desire.

These searches are often fruitless because there is no one right way and the right key is held in everyone's hands. Like most managers, you know the nuts and bolts of the present work you perform. What you need most, I feel certain, is help at the emotional level, in the psychology of understanding the modern concept of leadership.

The search for a magic way to succeed in the business world can be deeply frustrating. You and I know many persons who have labored at the same job year after year, who have never seemed to make a consistent effort to get out of their rut and move upward toward bigger things. We wonder why these people have been so afraid of trying to get further ahead that they settled for second or third best out of life. In some cases, they came to realize that they had reached the outer limits of their capabilities and could go no farther. But in other cases, they simply gave in to their frustration, convinced that the deck was stacked against them.

You can get everything out of the business world that you want, but there is no easy, magical way to do it. You can rise to the top with the help of other people and in spite of other people. You are an individual unto yourself, and, as it is with all things peculiar to you, it is certain that you will already have begun to develop your own leadership style.

What you seek at each level of your rise to the top is to harmonize your leadership style with the requirements of each position. You do this best when you exert a cool control over yourself and a steady influence over other people to achieve the productivity and results that top management wants of you at each level of responsibility.

There are no electrifying nuts and bolts of advice in this book that alone will assure your success. What you will find is fundamental but enormously effective information to which you can supply the magic of your own enthusiasm and consuming interest, with the result that you can begin almost immediately to experience an amazingly powerful thrust upward in your ambitions, your achievements, and your successes.

Charles C. Vance

*Manager Today,
Executive Tomorrow*

CHAPTER ONE

The Psychology of Measuring the Impact of Others in Your World

Your steady rise in the business world is inescapably related to your ability to cope successfully with a tremendous variety of problems. Some of your thorniest problems are those caused by other people. Coping successfully with problems of this nature is difficult unless you understand some of the basic psychology of measuring the emotional impact that others have on you and of assessing your reactions to what other people have done, or not done.

The problems that are not *people-caused* are the easiest ones to handle. A sudden rainstorm that catches you out in the open, a car that won't start, a big snowstorm that stops all traffic, an airplane that you missed, an alarm clock that didn't go off even though you set it properly. These you can quickly rise above because there is nothing personal about them. Irritating, yes, but they fade quickly.

People-problems rarely fade quickly. Why? Your emotional response shoots up during people-problems because you have a large residue of people-oriented hostility in you. This hidden hostility triggers either a rapid resentment or a flame of fear, depending on the situation. Emotions such as hostility like to hang around for awhile.

You are buffeted about each day by people-problems. A few days may be uneventful; you can be thankful for such tranquil periods. But you are always among people, and the winds and tides of human behavior are such that you can't predict from where the personality storms will come or how light or intense they will be.

The people you work with obviously have a great impact on you. They affect your world more than you like. You can gradually fall apart emotionally if you fail to understand the basic phenomena of the hidden impacts of human interrelations. Understanding yourself is your greatest challenge. Understanding other people and their many different impacts on you is your next greatest challenge.

We'll take a comprehensive look at you in the chapters that follow. In this chapter let's open some doors, raise some windows, and get a good view of the "others" in your world.

What attitudes should you have about the others?

Why should you have any special attitudes about other people in your organization? Won't the ordinary run-of-the-mill attitudes do?

Yes and no. Ordinary attitudes will do fine if you don't care to go very far in the business world. Special attitudes *are* necessary if you want to become a top executive.

The way you regard the people with whom you work is an inescapable part of your life-style as an executive-in-training. You can cope with other people only to the extent that you develop a set of personal-attitude ground rules. These rules will work best for you during your entire business life if they are based on practical reality, not on wishful thinking.

That sounds reasonable, doesn't it? But what is *practical reality?*

It's not kidding yourself about where you stand with other people. It's stripping away all the misconceptions you have about how you think you appear to other people and gaining an unobstructed look at yourself the way they really see you.

When you begin to strengthen certain of your attitudes in relation to "the others," you simultaneously begin to understand yourself through their eyes. You're not blocked by a deceptive image of how you think you are coming across to them but are armed instead with a more realistic appraisal of how you *are* coming across to them.

Let's take a look at some of these special attitudes:

1. *You know that from birth to death you are alone.* From the moment your heart starts to the instant it stops, you are locked within yourself. You travel the path of your life all by yourself. You can exist for periods of time without another soul near you, but you exist best when you are with people and are adjusted to them, when you are capable of adjusting to the many different types you meet. You can't get out of yourself. No way. You come into this life by yourself, you live within yourself, and when you leave you depart alone. That's attitude No. 1.

2. *Despite what you deeply believe, you know that no one you meet in your entire life owes you anything.* One of the greatest fantasies people possess is that their parents, their family, their boss, their friends, the people with whom they work owe them something. Individuals feel that they are owed recognition, respect, loyalty, devotion, obedience, attention, love, affection, sympathy, understanding—all that and more. Each individual does receive some of these wonderful gratuities, but they are freely given, not owed. Think about it for a long time. *Why* should people owe you any uplifting emotional response? They don't. That's attitude No. 2.

3. *Change is taking place before your eyes and you welcome it.* Change goes down hard. No one, but no one, really welcomes

change without constantly prompting themselves to open up their arms and receive it. We all prefer the familiar. We all like standard routines. We like everything in its place without disruption. We all are reluctant to dive wholeheartedly into new things. When changes arrive, say in fashions, we resist them until we no longer can. Then we hop on the bandwagon. *Most* of us do, anyway. There are always some strong holdouts for the status quo. There is a saying, "Change is permanent, and permanency is temporary." In business, many changes are accepted only after a long period of time. *You* can't grow, you can't develop into a top executive, unless you understand that change is always underway in a myriad of forms. You learn to welcome it because you know it is a way of the world, a way of humanity. That's attitude No. 3.

4. *You know that a life without trouble is impossible.* Have you ever read an outstanding novel that had *no* conflict in its pages? Have you ever seen a good stage play or movie that had no troubles for its characters? Have you ever had a friend who somehow escaped having difficulties? Have you ever heard of a corporation or a business organization that did not experience some trying times? Never! Trouble involving you comes in many forms, but it comes most often from the interactions between persons. Someone goofs, makes an incredible mistake, simply wasn't thinking, hated someone else, was strongly jealous, was ignorant of the facts, acted rashly, acted out of the wrong motivation, made a disastrous decision. We would all appreciate trouble-free days. Sometimes we have them, but not in a long string. Troubles come whether we want them or not. They are impersonal. You understand this. That's attitude No. 4.

5. *You accept the fact that you're going to win some and lose some.* The younger you are the more you're convinced that you'll win all the marbles. The intense desire to succeed that you have when you start on your first job or two gets whittled down after you discover you can't win them all. I think that all of us suffer this shock, the jolt of discovering that *other people* win some of

the promotions, pay raises, better transfers, approvals of the bosses. No matter how hard we try, how good our efforts, we sometimes lose. Who hasn't felt comparative envy on seeing a co-worker, another manager, a friend, or just someone we know, get a bigger salary, grab a more exciting job, have their name in the newspaper for something special that they did? As you labor in the vineyards of business, you come to understand that the only thing wrong with your attitude about winning all the marbles was that you anticipated too much. Life doesn't work that way for everyone. For a few chosen "lucky ones" (who actually make their own breaks) perhaps, but most of us win some and lose some. We learn to be happy when we win and philosophical (as opposed to being hurt or bitter) when we lose. That's attitude No. 5.

6. *You realize that the word "progress" has different meanings.* So you're convinced you're not making the progress you deserve? Well, what does the word "progress" mean to you? How do you measure it? By how fast you get promotions? By a steady series of pay raises? By comparing how well you do to how poorly some others you know are doing? Progress can be measured only by looking backward. Or so you think. The mature way to look at progress is to check where you are now *against* where you want to be five and ten years ahead and to examine how well you're preparing yourself to get there. Progress isn't history, progress is the future. Progress isn't you measured against someone else. It is your slow, steady movement toward realistic goals, goals that are reasonably attainable, not pure dream stuff. You learn not to hurt yourself by a false measurement of progress. That's attitude No. 6.

7. *No matter what other people do, you never stop learning.* You see other managers taking it easy, coasting on the job. You see them immersed in the office politics game. You see them getting by more on show than on go. You're strongly tempted to move with the tide yourself. But you have something going for you that they don't—a desire to get to the top. You can't get to

the top unless you have the skills to handle the jobs at that level. You take night courses, you read the right textbooks, you pore through the appropriate trade journals, you take on extra assignments to gain experience. You keep your mind busy absorbing more and more information. You understand that learning is a lifetime task and that when you stop learning you simply float where you are. Learning new management techniques in many areas is difficult, but it is one of the exotic fuels that propels you upward in the organization. Let the others run their own show, you'll run yours. That's attitude No. 7.

8. *You choose enthusiasm instead of pessimism.* Your company isn't going any place. The management is sealed off and gutless. Other companies are better places to work in. No one cares about the little guy. You can't get anywhere unless you know somebody at the top. You hear these bitches and knocks from the doomsayers. Being pessimistic is a way of life with a lot of people. You can't change most of them no matter how hard you try. Pessimism is four flat tires that leave you stalled alongside the highway while everyone else goes zipping by. They go by because they are buoyed up with enthusiasm and optimism. Study the men and women who have made it to the top. You'll see that most of them avoided the dangers of negative thinking. You refuse to let others flatten your tires. Enthusiasm is a priceless rolling power, and it is yours by choice. Let the others grumble and complain, bitch and gripe, knock and tear. You're going places, and enthusiasm helps you move faster. That's attitude No. 8.

These are a few of the strong attitudes that are structural members of your personal ground rules for moving up to the executive suite.

They are strengths that sustain and cushion you during the trials of a working day. They help you to control who you are and how you intermesh with other people. Like everything else in life, it is a matter of choice. You can choose to let other people influence you with *their* ways and *their* emotions. Or you can choose to develop your own attitudes that will push you upward to where you want to be.

Managers don't get to the executive level if all they have are secondhand attitudes. They get there with solid ones of their own choosing.

Why do they do what they do?

In all your life, you'll never fully understand everyone. Nor will you fully understand why people do the things they do. Why do some people become alcoholics? Why do others carry on affairs? Why do some tell barefaced lies? Why are others not dependable when with a little effort they could be?

The list of human frailties goes on endlessly. Almost everyone you meet has a blank spot where a good character trait should be. Why are people deceitful, dishonest, slow to respond to challenge, uneager to take on new work, boastful without reason, pompous, vain, unreliable, narrow-minded, depressed, humorless, and all the rest of the sorry deficiencies?

Because they belong to the human race.

So do *you*, and the chances are that you have some really great blank spots of your own. Who hasn't? But *you* not only have the opportunity to fill in these spots with the good character traits; you have the compelling drive to do so. That's like spotting you 20 yards in the 100-yard dash.

Working with other people is never easy because of these human frailties. The mild-mannered manager may become testy and bitter upon realizing that a long-awaited promotion is never going to come. The hotshot who moved along rapidly for years now feels cruelly held back by an inconsiderate superior. The frustration is difficult to control.

Most of us will never understand the full range of human emotions. Every adult is a long-range projection of a childhood. The emotions which start in you while you are still in the womb grow with your body. They are fashioned over the years by the experiences peculiar to you, the owner of the body: your so-called "childhood environment"; the influences of your parents, brothers and sisters, relatives, schoolmates; the good or bad economics of your early years; your impressions of your peers and of older persons.

I've seen the term "residual immaturities" used in describing why we still march to the drumbeat of our childhood experiences. It means we are still governed, no matter what our age, by hidden emotions that date back to our earliest years, The love-hate balance by which we measure everyone with whom we come in contact is rigidly set in childhood.

As adults, we measure out either some form of love or some form of hate to everyone we know. The love may be in the form of friendship, respect, admiration, adoration, sexual conquest, whatever. The hate may be in the form of contempt, envy, distrust, jealousy, cruelty, ridicule, criticism, avoidance, scorn, or any of a hundred shades of dislike.

The closer you are to people the more intense is the flame of love or hate. The more distant you are from people the less inclined you are to feel any form of love or hate for them. Strangers receive more courtesy and interest from us because at the point of meeting they are distant from us. We don't know them well enough to hate or love them. When we *do* come to know them, we assign them to one or the other side of our love-hate measure.

In the close confines of an office or a manufacturing facility there are no strangers. Everyone is known. The beginner, after a few months, is no longer a stranger.

So the residual immaturities come strongly into play. Beginners find themselves liked by some and ignored by others. They are being received or turned off according to the concealed emotional responses they evoke in the people around them.

By no means are *you* forgotten in this human process. You are affected by these emotional responses, often without even being aware that you are. Like the rest of us, you tend to feel that everyone you meet is a rational, clear-thinking individual who will see at once that you are an extraordinary person and will accord you the recognition you believe you deserve. While this is the way you feel, your growing mature sense informs you that being warmly accepted by other people is far more difficult and complicated than you had realized.

You know you can't get anywhere in the business world without becoming a manager of other peoples' work. Your task, then, is to understand the reasons *why* people do the things they do.

Let's explore some of the more popular forms of far-out, mixed-up, kooky, often-laughable, often-sad human conduct.

A look at the "fits"

You know quite a few people who seem to fill the description of a person well in control of himself, or herself, and of life. These are the "fits."

They are individuals with ambition who are working hard to be successful. They are like you in many respects. On the surface they appear to have it made or to be in the process of making it.

Are they?

Scratch any of these "fits" and you'll see many a flea of discontent and uneasiness hop off. These fine people (and they are good people) have all the emotional problems you or anyone else has. They simply are more capable of concealing them or controlling them. They have learned to cope more effectively with them, *but they still must cope*.

The "fits" have done very well in overcoming many of their residual immaturities, their childhood hang-ups. They've become business-wise, human relations-wise, tolerant of themselves and of others. Still they are never completely free of emotional flare-ups. They can be pinged by depression, dislike, anger, jealousy, resentment, at any moment.

Your relations with the "fits" go very well as long as you do not disturb any of the areas where they have inadequate control.

What makes it difficult for you is that they *are* expert at concealing their true emotions. You often don't know you've stepped on a sore emotional toe. They don't always let you know.

Be careful with the "fits." You can sense after a while whether or not you're being accepted by them. Your basic rule is never to believe that a man or a woman is what you see, no matter how fit they appear to be in mastering life's challenges. Believe what they *do*, not what they say.

If they *do* things that indicate you are "in" with them, then you have little to worry about. If they do *not* do these things, then somehow you've stepped on their sore emotional toe. You'll probably never find out how you managed to do this.

A look at the "misfits"

Sometimes it seems as though half the people you know are in this group. These are the real human failures. They are so rigid and limited in their thinking that they can't wholeheartedly accept delegated work. They can't form lasting friendships at the office. They can't contribute practical ideas and suggestions except in rare instances.

The "misfits" dread to make a definite decision. They are afraid of responsibility because it pushes them up where people can see them. They prefer to be invisible, to be left out of decision making.

They accept the piddling jobs, the boring drudgery of the same work day after day. They are misfits in the general scheme of business because they lack ambition, enthusiasm, and engaging personalities. They are not, in other words, management material.

They are there, in their monotonous sameness, and they represent a minor problem to you. They're not going anywhere, and if you play them wrong they can hamper *your* progress. You must manage them. Despite their reluctance to be managed by anyone, *you* can find ways to do it effectively.

Put yourself in their place. What would you want from you?

You would like to be noticed, to be made to feel necessary and important to the group's work, to be appreciated and not be shut out. Life has already fashioned you into a misfit, a person who feels cut off from the others. You would want your manager to lessen this pain, this embarrassment, this discomfiture.

There you have it. Satisfy this unspoken need for some recognition, no matter how small, and you can harmonize most of these unfortunate people into your working group.

I say "unfortunate" because they don't want to be misfits. They simply have never been able to unlock their drive-ahead emotions even though they've held the key right in their hands.

You're far more fortunate. *Your* drive-ahead emotions are unlocked and you're going places.

The "we-were-here-ahead-of-you" people

Everyone has had the nonpleasurable experience of meeting these people. Rarely do you go into an organization at the same time that everyone else does. Usually someone has been there ahead of you. Systems and practices have been developed, social structures have been built, likes and dislikes have been crystalized. Sides have been chosen.

If you're replacing someone who has left, for whatever reason, you have a problem, the extent of which depends on how popular that someone was.

If you're occupying a newly created position, you have the problem of coping with the disgruntled people who felt *they* should have been named to the job. Their hostility is only slightly concealed.

Some of them go out of their way to tell you how tough they had it before you came. They imply that you haven't suffered as they have. Others form a sort of clique of oppressed persons. They "include you out" because you didn't suffer the indignities to which they feel they were subjected.

There is a tyranny to this sort of "we-were-here-ahead-of-you" thing. It is unfair to you, coming in either as an addition to the group or as its manager, to be subjected to this tyranny. There isn't much you can do about it. That's the way people are, and only time and good conduct on your part will erase their initial coldness to you. Use the "this-too-will-pass" approach. Expect it and don't allow it to get under your skin.

The ones with the competitive neurosis

You'll suffer nightmares if you take these competitive people more seriously than you should. You must be serious about them if they are your equals and are bucking for the next promotion —the one you're bucking for. You must be serious about them also if they're a notch or two below you and are anxious to get your present job. Whether they're equals or risers, they represent trouble to you. But it is a type of trouble that you can handle. You don't really expect to have the field all to yourself, do you? Would a job be any good if no one else wanted it?

The way to handle competitors is to remind yourself of these facts:

1. For any worthwhile position there are bound to be others who *want* it whether they are qualified or not.

2. The competition is hottest between the ones who are *best* qualified. Top management ordinarily isn't out of its collective mind. You're up against good individuals in the final analysis.

3. Those who get the positions do so because they have convinced the top brass that they're the ones who can *produce the most*.

4. The *competition* boils down to a demonstration by you and your competitors that you *can produce* the type of management that qualifies you for promotion.

5. *You win* whether you get this particular promotion or not. You win because the competition is snapping behind you, forcing

you to remember every day that victory goes to the one who plans better and performs better than the others in the pack.

Who likes competition? No one! We all would like cheap shots at every promotion. We fantasize about being called in and told *we've been chosen* for the big job. We'll walk on air. Everyone will be delighted, our spouse, children, parents, friends, the group . . . hold it. The group?

Our competitors will like it? Hold it! No way. You've just made stronger enemies out of competitors.

The competitive neurosis is a major disease in American business. The more you understand about it the more you can use it to help you move up toward the top.

The American ethic that each person must become a respectable success is deeply rooted in our culture. In order to satisfy the "my-child-can-be-President-of-the-United-States" syndrome of parents affected by this disease, many a child develops a compulsive drive, often mindless, to get as far as he or she can in the world.

It is fanned by some wives and husbands who want more of the material things of life, and by children who prove to be extremely expensive to raise and send to school. It is oxygenated by our social structure in which status is seldom based on what a person is, but on what a person owns. It is festered by emotional disturbances within the people who are engaged in the competitive struggle to win the goodies of the material world.

How do you escape the bad side of the American ethic and use the good side for your benefit? The answer is so simple you won't believe it.

Let the *others* be affected by the competitive neurosis. Your way of escape is to see yourself as a realistic campaigner for bigger and better jobs, *but not on an emotional level*. Refuse to dislike the others you're struggling against. Refuse to compare yourself to them as if you were all "souped-up" automobiles of different makes.

Stick with your game plan of moving ahead. If a competitor

makes it to one of the notches you had your eyes set on, then set your eyes on another notch and work for that. By failing to become rigidly wrapped in the narrow confines of one competitive struggle, you free yourself to look up and beyond, and to prepare yourself for bigger things.

Will it work? Try it.

What to do about unavoidable conflicts

It is unrealistic to expect that you can go along year after year without meeting someone whose chemistry is absolutely wrong for your chemistry.

Really serious personality conflicts are rare, but they do happen, and the best of us may become embroiled. Let's say this happens to *you*. Someone is making trouble and you're in the center of it.

Rule One is, "When a storm threatens, run to safety!" The subelements of this single-minded rule are these:

1. You'd be out of your mind to try to slug it out.

2. For a while put as much space between the two of you as you can manage each day. Avoid any prolonged exposure to this threat to your security. Your job is to put out the fire, not fan it.

3. Do some serious thinking about why this chemical imbalance started in the first place. Try to trace it back to its beginning. *Why* does this person regard you in an antagonistic light? What did you do? What did she or he do? What was said or done somewhere along the line that got it started?

4. Don't flatter yourself that you're the angel and the other person is the devil. You did or said *something*. Get a grip on whatever this was and start to work smoothing this over.

5. Don't wait. Get busy right away. Work out a conversation plan to start easing the situation. Once you are sure of yourself and have a sensible (as against an emotional) idea of where things went wrong, find ways to talk about it. Sometimes a direct

approach works. Sit together in one office and say something like, "I've been thinking about the problem between us, and I can see that I got off on the wrong foot with you. Care to talk about it with me?" You know something about this person's personality; will the direct approach work? Perhaps you must use the indirect approach, finding ways to compliment the other on past accomplishments. You ignore the previous harshness and act as if nothing has happened. But you present things to approve in you, not things to find more trouble with.

6. Whichever approach you use, you must get your relationship on a new track. It won't be easy; don't expect it to be. Nor can you do it in one day. You're in a personality bind with this person, and it is up to you to get out of it. Don't tell yourself it's the other person who should be making the first moves. You'll wait a long time. Get busy on your own, and don't miss a legitimate opportunity to bring the two of you closer. Outright flattery will kill you. A time and place for everything, *remember*.

7. Look for the lesson in this personality conflict. The things you said and did rubbed this person the wrong way. Will you do it to others? You can't afford to have anyone down on you. Learn your lesson; one is there for you to learn. And don't get caught in this type of unhappy situation again.

Being aware of the dangers the others create for you

A harsh personality conflict is one thing. It can scare the daylights out of you before you get it smoothed over to where it no longer is a threat to you.

There are other dangers. Why do I use the word "dangers"? Because many people have found themselves "not going anywhere" for the basic reason that they thought they were something special and that no one, but no one, would make trouble for them. That attitude is so simple-minded I won't comment on it.

The more energetic managers are, the more they have on the

ball, the more they perform, the more they are able to move ahead, the more often they are right than wrong, the more some people want to bring them down.

The amazing thing is that most of these people don't mean it personally. That's right. If this manager is *you*, it means you are highly visible. *You* are doing things many of them can't do. *You* are succeeding where many of them are wallowing in self-pity and injured resentment. *You* are a moving target, and the temptation to potshot at you is irresistible.

They'll take cheap shots at anyone who looks as though he's going to make it while it looks as though they won't. It is a nasty part, a sick area, of human nature. You can't do much to change it. You *can* do something about your particular situation. Here's a checklist:

1. Awareness that the problem exists for you is the starting point. Don't kid yourself that you're such a sweet person they'll give you a pass. No way.

2. Make a list of those above you, at your own level, and a bit below you, of all the people you feel might fit into this "teardown" category. Who are in an influential spot to hurt you, no matter how high or low their position in the organization? Keep this list up to date.

3. Make an effort to spend some time with all of them occasionally. Have lunch with them, a coffee break, stop and talk to them in the hallways, drop into their offices or stop by at their desks. Find out about their families, their hobbies, their likes and dislikes. Build a storehouse of information about them.

4. Now you're well armed. They aren't strangers to you. Just regular human beings, who, if you avoid them, can be dangerous to you with their behind-your-back potshots. You're not going to tempt them. By taking yourself to them, by talking to them at their level, you reduce their feeling that *somehow you are a threat to them*. You know you're no threat to them, but they often don't see it that way. They can peg you as a hotshot, an office politi-

cian, a phoney, all that. They can undercut your growing reputation as a doer. You remove yourself as a threat to them by showing them *you are interested in them as individuals*. The more they begin to see you as a sincere manager who has a deep sense of responsibility, who wants to move ahead, and who has ability, the less they see you as a moving target to be resented, feared, and torn down.

The biggest danger they can collectively pose for you is to create an impression that "you can't get along with anyone." The next danger is that they can establish a feeling that "something is wrong with you." They can hamper the best of your assignments. They can create small situations which you spend a lot of time trying to clear up.

You get the picture. If you don't, you're not executive material.

Why you must write off some people

Despite all your efforts, some people just aren't going to cotton to you. Why?

They have some deep-seated emotional problem and you, little old you, make the problem worse. You remind them of someone they really detest. You're of the wrong faith, the wrong color, the wrong background, whatever.

You've made the effort to get to them, and they didn't respond. What do you do? You write them off. There is a difference between trying to get along with people and lowering yourself too far in the attempt.

The rule: Stay away from them. Be courteous and considerate when you come in contact with them. Don't let them steam you even in the smallest way with their rudeness or coolness. But limit your time with them to the smallest possible amount.

With a few people of this type you just can't make it. There's no sense in knocking yourself out trying to.

How many true friends will you acquire?

How many fingers do you have on your right hand?

You must go through life *trying* to make friends. It's an essential part of your from-manager-to-executive training. You must settle for something a bit less, acquaintances by the score and friends by the fingers.

Do you know the difference? Friends are those wonderful people who find you interesting, perhaps colorful, fun to be with, a source of inspiration and enthusiasm, and no threat to themselves.

Acquaintances are not so deeply interested in you. They don't find you so colorful, nor so much fun to be with, they don't get too much from you, and you might be a threat to them sometime, somewhere. They tolerate you more than they like you. They're just a shade careful when they're with you, a bit on guard, They don't resent you or worry deeply about you. It's just that they're far more interested in themselves than in you.

Real friends give you a lot of themselves. They forgive, forget, make allowances, have a good humor about your successes.

Acquaintances give little and couldn't care less about *your* successes.

Think about all the acquaintances you've made and think about the people you regard as your "true friends." I'm right, am I not?

What makes the business world so complicated?

Emotions.

Some people harbor the illusions that the business world is well organized, that executives always know what they're doing, that difficulties arise from nonhuman sources, that "teamwork" exists in a solid American way, and that business enterprises are based on the need to serve the general public.

That these illusions have a strong element of truth to them does not diminish the fact that they are illusions after all.

For if all this were 100 percent true, why is the business world so complicated? Certainly the technology in which we're immersed makes it complicated. Certainly both the internal rules and regulations and those of the various governments complicate the business life. Certainly competition causes great difficulties.

Despite all these pressures, business of any kind could be run beautifully, almost effortlessly, if the disruptive emotional factors of its executives, managers, and employees were eliminated.

But it would be enormously dull!

The disruptive emotions that complicate the business world are the same ones that complicate our personal lives.

Executives fight for control of the company—to gain the mantle of power over others so that that same power won't be used against them.

Managers fight against one another to win the next promotion, to gain more of the "power" rewards—more money, more prestige, more opportunities to run things, more of the satisfactions of success.

Employees fight against one another for a bit of "power" leverage of their own, an office to oneself, a better boss to work under, new office equipment that denotes special attention, any type of "one-upmanship."

Companies fight against one another (their executives do) not so much to drive one another out of business as to keep from being forced out of business themselves.

So the business world is a power fight from beginning to end. It is a power fight a lot of people lose because they don't know the ground rules. The No. 1 ground rule is that everyone seeks something for himself or herself. The No. 2 ground rule is that someone always wants the same thing someone else has. The

No. 3 ground rule is that no one goes about this combat lackadaisically or disinterestedly; they're in it tooth and nail, bite for bite, stab for stab. The No. 4 ground rule is that in any power struggle the entire orchestra of emotions is in full beat. The background beat is strong, forceful, sometimes awesome in its impact.

The disruptive emotions of greed, vanity, hate, jealousy, pettiness, vindictiveness, maliciousness, even cruelty, exist in us all. In the business world, where so much is at stake, these emotions take on a special sharpness, a special cruel thrust, a special knife cut of defeat, if allowed to run unchecked against you.

When you deal with the others in your corner of the business world, you are really dealing with their emotions. Remember that and it will help make the business world a bit less complicated for *you*.

How these complications fashion your life-style

You want to win. And you know you can't win unless you are able to get other people to work effectively. It comes down to how well you develop your capabilities of managing other people. Managing their emotions, you might say. These capabilities become your life-style in the business world.

In learning how to manage others you are forced to learn how to manage yourself. The two go hand in hand. People who can successfully manage themselves and other people are on their way to becoming successful executives. That's a winning life-style.

The techniques for turning the impact of others into an upward force for you

It isn't all that difficult.

So what if "the others" have cutting emotions? So what if the business world is "power"-complicated? So what if we live in a roller coaster life of changes? That is the way things are (and always have been), and we must accept it.

There are many techniques for you to use in turning the impact other people have on your personal world into positive values for you. Others have done it. You can do it.

Let me offer the following list of techniques for your consideration. Some may work splendidly for you. Others may bomb out. But as you read them you'll see a broad strain of effort on your part that will, over the long haul, enable you to win more than you lose. And that is what you want.

1. *Look for the pleasant contacts.* In every office and plant there are people whom you'll like, people who will give a bit more to you than they'll take. Refresh yourself with these wonderful people as often as you can. They compensate for "the others" who aren't so pleasant. Go out and develop strong acquaintanceships with them. There may even be a friend hidden in the pile.

2. *Don't believe what you see.* People let you see only so much of their true selves, and you can be fooled if you believe only what you see of them. A grumpy person may actually be a fine but lonely person trying to call attention to himself. A fine person (on the surface) may actually be a bitter grouch who in public is able to conceal his constant resentment. A flirty secretary may actually be a prude trying to act the role she believes is expected of her. Almost all people spend time desperately trying to conceal their true identity. They're playing a part, an actor's role, in the drama of the business world. Don't be taken in. Look for the clues which indicate what they *really* are like inside. Like all actors they'll forget their lines once in a while, and then you'll catch a glimpse of who they are.

3. *Forget the "fan-club" tendency.* As a manager of other people you'll have a tendency to think they form a sort of a fan club, cheering you on to greater heights, applauding your successes. Stay out of this trap. Some of them may actually like you well enough to be cheered mildly by your winning ways; most of

them couldn't care less about you. They want you to *think* they do, and they'll artfully pretend they regard you as wonderful. If you fall for it, you'll fall for a three-dollar bill as well.

4. *Let them have their sillinesses.* Peculiarities abound in human nature. Some people talk too much, others seldom open their mouths. There are those who insist on telling you everything their children do. You run into braggarts, pornographic hounds, old-joke tellers, flashy-jewelry collectors, sly manipulators, those who own expensive cameras and don't know how to use them, those who buy expensive homes and foreign automobiles they can't afford, the Glitter Gulch swingers who pose on the bar stools, and the like. All this is the salt and pepper and other condiments of human existence. It is merely a "front" that they develop to impress themselves first and you second. They'd be pretty dull without the camouflage, so let them have it.

5. *Keep yourself turned on.* In life's course you'll shift and change in your needs of others. You exist in a sea of other people. At times you'll want to escape from them, and after you escape you'll want to be back in their midst. If you close yourself off from them when you feel depressed or disenchanted, your aloofness will tend to turn them against you. Most of us are good at imagining the others "are against us," but this is still only imagination. It becomes a reality when you turn yourself off from them and they reciprocate. As in the laws of physics, any human force is met with a counterforce.

6. *Keep your "recognition spotlight" turned on.* Everyone else is just as human as you are. They want to be noticed; they dread being ignored. Whatever position they hold, low, middle, high, they want you to pay some attention to them. It is your job to get work done by motivating other people to do it. You simply can't do it all by yourself. Sharpen your "people-oriented attitude" by remembering each day that every person has a desire for distinction of one sort or another. Find the incentive for each person in your group. It may be a pay raise, but more ordinarily it is a personal climate that you establish, a climate in which they

receive a pat on the back when they do good work. Sympathy and understanding are important to people when they're caught up in a problem. They can sense that you accept them and that you're pleased to have them as part of your group.

7. *Use the power of your insight.* Giving proper recognition to your subordinates and others in the office or plant is one thing. Using your insight allows you to determine their strong points and weak points. They'll respond more to you in your efforts to motivate them to do better work if you build up their better image of themselves. Assign them activities where you know they have strength; don't give them jobs to do in areas where they are weak unless you have time to work with them in overcoming that weakness. Help them satisfy their need to succeed, and you'll gain some credit from them by understanding what it is they want to achieve in their jobs. No one is just a simple working mechanism. Each person you meet is an incredibly complicated computer bank of nerves, programmed to be suspicious of change, to be filled with worry and insecurity, unwilling to be dominated. People are easily angered at not being filled in about what's going on, frustrated by their inability to perform as well as they would like, supersensitive about making decisions, unable to see clearly where they should work to improve themselves or sometimes dully complacent and pleased with themselves. When your insight is at a peak you understand how complex human behavior is and you use the strong and weak points of your people to manage them wisely and effectively. And you are the winner because you allow them to win as well.

8. *Get to the heart of what grabs them.* The reality of good management is built on your ability to make your people feel a solid part of your group. You can grab them right where they live by doing these things:

a. Create an atmosphere of two-way communications. You develop this atmosphere so that you can talk to them and they can talk freely to you in a spirit of mature give and take. You learn what they're thinking (and feeling). When they're talking, listen to them. Not a surface listening but a gut listening. You seldom kid anyone by pretending to listen.

b. Give them a number of incentives. If you make it an either-or incentive you may lose them. Offer them several incentives for doing a better job or for carrying out a specific assignment. Show them that you're interested in helping them achieve goals that are meaningful to *them,* not just to you.

c. Instill your confidence in them. They're watching you constantly. If you're optimistic, enthusiastic, confident, it will rub off on them. You manage best when you instill a sense of importance in the individuals under you, when you build up their good opinion of themselves and of the place where they work. Your people want to feel that they're going somewhere. They feel this most when they see that *you* are convinced the entire group is pulling together, is making progress, is winning out.

d. Give some of yourself to them. Training the others is an essential ingredient in your rise to an executive's job. Despite any irrational attitudes they may have about working for a living, they can be trained, they can learn new ways—if you give some of yourself to them to help them master the new methods. When they show that they're troubled by an assignment, ask them what you can do to help them over the hurdles. Lording your superiority over them will get you nowhere. Use the question technique. When they're puzzled, ask, "How about if we tried it this way? Do you think it would work?" Asking their opinions prompts a response in them. They'll see that you are sincerely trying to help them develop their talents. That's what they want. You gain more of their loyalty and respect. Their work levels will rise when you are specific about what you want done, when you indicate your willingness to train them, to help them along, to show them exactly what authority they have, when you remove any roadblocks in their way (such as too much work to be done in too short a time), and when you give them credit for the work they do effectively.

e. Retain a grasp of reality. Management of other people is the most difficult task any of us can imagine. Your subordinates never see you the way you see yourself. The reality of working with others is based on your refusal to believe that they see you as you think you are. *That* illusion can wreck you. Try to see yourself as they do, through their eyes. That is the reality of the business world.

f. Keep your irritations to yourself. It's so easy to bawl out a subordinate when things go wrong. It's the worst thing you can do in most cases. If you're under pressure, working long days against a tight timetable, don't pop your cork when things go wrong. Things are *always* going wrong. Looking for a fall guy or a whipping boy may be tempting, but you'll defeat yourself. You can't throw the fire and brimstone of your temporary anger at anyone and not have it come back to haunt you later. Why cause yourself more trouble? Keep your irritations to yourself. Go somewhere and cool off. Tamper with a person's good opinion of himself by clouding up and raining all over him, even when he deserves it, and you've made an enemy. Your job is to make successful subordinates, not enemies.

How other people help you rise to the top

You're being watched. Top management is looking at you every day and measuring you for that big promotion. What do they measure you by?

1. You are a person who gets things done.
2. You get things done by motivating other people to help you do them.
3. You are an accomplished organizer not only of your own work but of the work of 'the others."
4. You accept responsibility and actually like being responsible for a heavy work load.
5. You are able to persuade "the o hers" to share some of that responsibility.

How can you become an executive unless you measure up to this management yardstick? How can you get anywhere in the business world without the ability to lead other people? Your success in working with "the others" is paramount in your rise toward the top. There is no other way. Understand that good management of "the others" *is* your stairway to the executive suite at the top, and you're well on your way there.

CHAPTER TWO

The Psychology of Knowing Yourself Better

So you think you know who you are!

You don't like yourself. You don't have all the confidence you need. You see others getting ahead and you feel you're falling behind. You're convinced that somewhere something went screwy and you're on the wrong path.

Welcome to the human race! We're all in the same boat. Very few people escape the ravages of negative thinking. Those who aren't consciously aware of it almost always have overcompensated for their unconscious feelings of this sort by finding some way "to come on strong."

In your lifetime you'll probably meet no more than a handful of men and women who truly like themselves as they are, who are contented with their lot in life, who possess plenty of confidence, who are satisfied with the progress they're making, and who think they've chosen the right path.

Why is this?

Our problems start early in life—and stay with us

Psychologists tell us that somewhere in childhood we become doubters. When we were infants we had power over others. We were supreme. When we cried we were picked up and cared for. When we were hungry we were fed. When we had a tantrum to attract attention we got attention.

As we moved out into life's stream we found we could lose a few as well as win a few. We discovered that our parents had *some* interests besides us. We learned that our schoolmates, some of them a lot smaller than we, could beat us at foot races, fist fights, jumping, climbing, staying out later to horse around, in tests, on and on.

We began to sense that the world was much bigger and tougher than we'd thought. There were older and larger people all around us, and they *knew* so much more than we did. They could *do* so much more. They possessed things like cars, motorcycles, boats, fishing tackle and sports gear of all kinds, and money. We had none of these things.

With our small size and limited grasp of things worldly, we began the process of learning to hate ourselves because we weren't really the center of the world after all.

In high school and college we had more shocks. We had to rely on the energy and talents within us, not on the supreme position that our fantasies had created for us. We were, at last, in full competition with others our own age. We were stunned by the knowledge that many of them were better in many areas than we were. Faced with excruciating challenges, we were floored emotionally when we didn't measure up to our expectations.

We made mistakes and regretted them in misery. We saw others whom we regarded as inferiors winning some of the prizes we wanted. As our horizons were pushed further back, we realized that we were a pretty small unit on the massive scale of humanity. We no longer were master of our infant world. We seemed to shrink in size, in meaning, and in importance.

By the time we entered "young adulthood" we no longer could avoid noticing the obvious. We simply were not all that we wanted to be. Our fantasies had been blasted to bits by reality. The struggle for our identity became intense, almost furious. Who, just who, were we? And where in this world were we going?

Virtually everyone goes through this identity crisis. Because it involves *us* we often are not even aware that we're in this crisis. Some enter its storm front earlier than others. Some remain engulfed in it all their lives.

After all that education, after learning how to cope with so many new situations and with the peculiarities of "the others," *you* inevitably came to a point in life, probably in young adulthood, when you:

1. Didn't like yourself "all that much."
2. Didn't feel so damned confident that you could make it.
3. Didn't feel you were getting ahead as fast as some of the others.
4. Didn't feel you'd gotten all the breaks to which you were entitled and *did* feel that somehow you were headed up the wrong creek.

And right now, today, who are you?

There are some basic facts of life that I can share with you in answering that question. Despite your reservations about yourself, *these facts* tell you the real story, not the one you imagine:

1. You are not radically different emotionally from any other "normal" person you've ever met.
2. You have come through much of the same maturing process that they have.
3. You ripened into *you* with your special characteristics, set of ethics, beliefs, code of behavior, reactions, and sensitivities. Though you differ from "the others" somewhat, you're not all

that much different. You just think you are because you can't get *inside* them and see how they tick emotionally.

4. For the remainder of your life, in one way or another, you will continue to cope with the questions, "Who am I?" and "Where am I going?"

5. One of the strangest emotional elements in your lifetime struggle to cope successfully with life's problems is that you feel *isolated* from the others. You see them, and, because you can't get inside and feel their emotions, you decide that they are coping with life more easily and effectively than you are. They look different, act differently, talk differently. They *must* have something special that you don't have. It never occurs to you that they see *you* and feel the same way toward you. When you compare yourself to others you'll always shortchange yourself, always feel a bit inferior. Your deep sense of isolation, caused by your absolute inability to get inside other people, forces you into a trap of complicated emotional tangles. You begin to envy others, resent them, be jealous, be afraid, be intimidated, be wary. And it's all such an uncalled-for waste of your energy and emotions.

6. The big sticker is that you never will really know yourself. You think so. What's new to learn about yourself? Plenty! You're a highly complex person. You're trying hard to cope with today's critical problems but *you're governed, in part, by things that happened many years ago.* You're still affected by the actions of people, some of whom are no longer near you or have been dead for years.

The fascinating thing is that with all your accumulated hang-ups and "puppet strings from the past" you've made progress in managing yourself and others.

You can make a great deal more progress if you come to better terms with your hang-ups, if you make a stronger effort to cut the "puppet strings" and to understand what makes you tick. Why do you do the things you do? Why do you feel the things you feel? Continually ask yourself these questions. Search yourself for the answers.

How can you control your less attractive emotions and make fuller use of your better ones so that you can move ahead? Are you ready to get to know yourself better? Let's go.

It takes more than just "because it's me"

Few people would attempt daring enterprises, high adventure of any sort, if they didn't feel that they possess *something special* which gives them a better chance to succeed.

This "because-it's-me" attitude has resulted in many successful adventures in the business world. It has also caused untold difficulties for individuals who recklessly went into enterprises equipped solely with this attitude and not with the accompanying skills, knowledge, and stamina. We're all equipped to some degree with this "because-it's-me" attitude, but we're fools if that's *all* we rely on to carry off a truly innovative, unique, or daring activity in the business world.

How do we handle this conflict? We all have the notion that everything we do is touched a bit with brilliance. Yet, when we look up and see the millions of persons in the world and the tremendous success that others have had, we feel the surging conflict of being emotionally deflated in the face of our "because-it's-me" attitude.

The answer is in two parts:

1. Don't dampen your "because-it's-me" attitude. It *is* you, after all. You *are* putting something of your own style into your work. Your big ideas may be rehashes of someone else's big ideas, but you're the one *doing something* about the situation. Keep the attitude good and strong because it is one of the hottest motivational forces you have going for you. Everyone else who succeeded (where others failed) used the attitude. Use yours.

2. Once you have your really innovative plan well in mind, pretend that *you* are your severest critic. What holes could be picked in it? Where could the plan be realistically criticized? If

you're at home, or in your office with the door closed, talk to yourself about the pros and cons of the idea. Question every part of it as if you had just heard of it for the first time. Play the game seriously, because this is where you stand or fall. If you can come up with honest answers to every question, then you *have* a good plan. You can go ahead and move it into the mainstream.

These two parts are priceless strategies for you. One buoys you up, the other strengthens your grip on the idea so that you don't come falling down when someone starts trying to shoot holes in it. You're ready for them, because you've anticipated their views.

Would you believe that most great management decisions are made pretty much along these lines by many, many top executives?

Getting a sharp, clear look at yourself

You're an executive-in-the-making. How do you *know* you've got what it takes? How much do you *believe* in yourself?

Let's run a little check on *what* you believe. What are your reactions to these sentiments, right or wrong?

1. It's a tough world. Everyone for himself. Dog eat dog.

2. No matter how hard you work or how much talent you have, it takes office politics to get ahead.

3. Top-management people look out for themselves. They don't give a damn about the managers down below.

4. They won't promote from within. They'll bring in somebody from the outside.

5. This place is a trap. There's nowhere to go. All the good spots are held by incompetents who'll live forever. (No one will get *them* to retire when they're sixty-five!)

If you feel these judgments are right, or nearly so, then you've got a problem. It's purely one of *negative thinking,* of seeing the worst instead of the best, of talking yourself out of really *trying* to move ahead.

These are standard "business sentiments," and you'll find somebody voicing them in almost every office or plant organization. They are a bad part of human nature. Bad because they cloud the pathway so that you can't see where you're going. They diminish your energies and confidence so that you slow down instead of speed up. You're the loser if you hang onto these negative sentiments.

Let's look at you from another angle. Try on these thoughts for size:

1. The trouble with the business world today is that it is big, enormously complicated, constantly changing, and yet not always appearing to change. When I try to come to grips with it, it slips out of my grasp. It just won't fit into any pattern I can easily understand.

2. I've been on this job a few years and I'm disillusioned, unhappy, bored. I feel they're taking advantage of me.

3. Working for a living is a rat race. I'm sick and tired of it. I'm wondering if there isn't some other place where I'd be better off, some other town, another company where I can make better progress.

4. I'm afraid that I won't end up with the things I want out of life. I thought at first that I could get them. Now I'm not so sure. Months go by, years slip away. I might not be able to get that big house or afford that trip to Europe. Forget that Corvette, too. What's going to happen to me and my family?

Pretty gloomy, aren't they?

Rarely does a person get very far into the business world before some form of disenchantment closes in. These four deadening thoughts and others like them are extremely prevalent among a great number of managers who have allowed themselves to sink into such disenchantment.

What's my point? Simply that *you* do not have to allow the

terrible grip of negative thinking to immobilize you. *You* do not have to permit disenchantment to rob you of your energies and confidence. Not in any way, shape, or form do *you* have to hurt yourself by believing in the *wrong things*.

Let's take a look at the positive side of you. Despite your human tendency to expect the worst and look at all the black sides, you are intellectually counterbalanced with enough positive attitudes to help you make progress toward the top.

How many of *these* statements and thoughts find their way into your comments and evaluations?

1. I'm in a race with time and the sooner I get busy programming myself to the top the faster I'll get there.

2. As a manager growing into an executive I expect to have adverse times. Knowing they're coming at any time equips me to deal with them.

3. As a manager, I'm a problem solver. If they didn't have problems they wouldn't need me to work things out. I can handle both the problems we anticipate and those we don't.

4. No one is in charge of my destiny except me.

5. I know that change is all about us and that I must continue to change over the years if I'm to reach the executive suite.

6. The last thing I want to be is a perfectionist, a person who can never be satisfied. I look for the satisfactory answer, not the perfect one.

7. People never improve if the world is soft on them. I know that I work better and accomplish more when the heat is on me. I don't resent the heat. It's pushing me upward, making a better problem solver out of me, forcing me to think and plan.

8. I know that I'm in a lifelong struggle to make it big in the business world, that there is no soft way to get the things I want. Only hard work and intelligent planning will get me the kind of money I want, the achievements, measure of success, security, the feeling of personal worth, and an enduring peace with myself.

You can't go around each day muttering these statements to yourself. But I'm sure they do *occur* as thoughts to you from time to time. Why don't they have more meaning then? Why don't they prompt you to work harder, make more progress, improve yourself more consistently? The answers lie in your own emotions.

The terrible grip of your emotions

Most people are a compromise. They don't start out that way, but they end up that way if they allow the terrible grip of their emotions to block them.

The tragedy is that most persons in this fix never admit to themselves that they *have* compromised. But the years pass and they begin to see, no matter how dimly, what has happened. *They sold themselves out.*

They come to understand that it wasn't someone else who clobbered them. They did it to themselves. They begin to mourn for "what might have been" if only they hadn't compromised with life. If only.

You're never completely out of the grip of your emotions, but you can loosen their bonds if you understand that *everyone* has problems and that you are *not* unique in having to cope with them.

Let's see what some of this coping includes.

1. I can force myself to *feel inferior* to others by worrying unnecessarily about losing my job, about what others think of me, about what my boss thinks of me, about the goofs I make, about a word of criticism I got recently, about how others are getting ahead faster than I am.

2. I can develop a real case of fatigue and turn out a lackluster performance by allowing anxiety to replace my confidence. I know that it can happen any day, at any time, if I allow myself to become a victim to my unconscious anxieties.

3. I can never stop trying to learn more about myself, what makes me tick. I have human conflicts, as everyone has, and these make it incredibly tough for me to "know myself." But I

can't give in to them blindly, I must keep working at trying to know myself.

4. If I want to become really flaky all I have to do is brood, feel self-contempt, become bitter, consider myself worthless, be sensitive about everything people say, and hate myself for the mistakes I made weeks, months, and years ago.

5. I know that if I allow myself to become self-centered I'll really isolate myself more from others. The isolation will cause me to drift along. I'll lose my powers of concentration, I'll become miserable, and greater tension will grab me.

6. When I feel myself becoming restless and discontented, I know I'm on the wrong path. I'm going down, not up.

Emotions are never easily controlled. Sometimes you have to use every bit of your mental strength to keep a bad emotion —hate, bitterness, envy, suspicion, jealousy, whatever—from taking you over. It's a lifetime task. You'll win some, lose some.

I have a friend who once said to me, "I wish I could shut part of my mind off at times, like a light switch, so I could allow my conscience some peace and quiet." It's a shame we don't have such a mind switch. We're left with our own conscious efforts at self-control.

How to use attitudes that help, not hurt

The perceptions about yourself that you develop as you mature in the business world show you that there are good, solid attitudes you can put to work for yourself.

This understanding helps you immeasurably in working out your own destiny. It takes you out of the Clownland of Wishful Thinking. It keeps you from constructing your own built-in failure contraptions.

Useful attitudes include these:

1. *Confidence* that I can organize my day professionally, as-

sign priority to the work items, cope with the problems so that they are solved, work out a plan to get the work done.

2. *Tolerance* of the daily stresses and conflicts, knowing that they are part of the business and will never go away unless I learn to live with them.

3. *Appreciation* of myself so that in a sense I am my own best friend, not my worst, and so that I can work to control my emotions because I don't want to hurt myself.

4. *Determination* to be myself, to build the best character I can, to use that solid character to become a reliable decision maker who gets things done.

5. *Aggressiveness* in exerting myself to take advantage of every opportunity to advance myself toward an executive's title.

6. *Sensitivity* to everyone and everything around me so that I'm alert, disciplined, and using my talents to the best of my ability.

7. *Desire* to banish my daily anxieties by identifying them as unreal emotions, and to eliminate hostilities toward myself and others which, if allowed to remain, are almost always blown up beyond reality.

8. *Enthusiasm* which puts some pep into my everyday work routine so that each day is a bit different from the others in spite of the same office confines, the same people, the similar problems.

9. *Conviction* that I am important, that I am doing an essential job with measurable results, that my bosses regard me as an accomplished person who is a self-starter, a doer, someone to bet on.

10. *Happiness* that I'm alive, feeling well, have a job, have opportunities to move up, have experience, have a home and a family, some free time, and wonderful motivations to become more successful in this complicated world.

Attitudes can cripple you or attitudes can push you forward. *You* are the one who decides which way to go. No one ever pushes you one way or the other. The choice is yours.

How to handle tension and anxiety

We create most of our tension and anxiety ourselves, without any help from others. We unrealistically expect things to go well. We expect, each day, to get along with ourselves, with those around us, and with our environment. Yet the great conflicts of life are centered in these three areas: you and yourself; you and those around you; you and wherever you happen to be on earth.

Tension has become a common word because we see it in TV commercials so much these days. Medical science has come to understand a great deal more about tension. Many persons are under tension, or stress if you prefer that word, all day long. Why?

Because few of use are as flexible as we think. We want things to go well, expect them to go well, and get uptight when they don't. In the business world most things just don't go the way you want them to all the time. If we're truly inflexible, we're unable to accept this. We remain uptight, in a state of tension, always half-mad about one thing or another.

We're unaware that *we* are causing the tension because of our unrealistic expectations. We think it is other people and other things that cause it. If we're in a big city, we run to catch a crowded commuter train, we're boxed into an office with many other persons, restaurants are jammed, service is slow, work piles up, things have gone wrong all day long. Tension!

You can rid yourself of most of your tension if you can accept several simple premises:

1. Things at the office don't go wrong just to cause *you* trouble. They go wrong, and you happen to be there to cope with them. You are being paid to cope with problems.

2. It is Neverneverland to *expect* things to go smoothly; you're asking for headaches when you expect to have a day clear of problems. No way.

3. It is a sharpening of your management abilities to persuade yourself to remain flexible and be objective (not subjective) about

the rush of work and the snarls and tangles that pop up all the time.

4. A look back at both your immediate history and your long-range history shows that no one you knew of any importance ever got anywhere without overcoming problem after problem. They remained loose and flexible and coped. They won out and rose to the top.

Tension comes in many disguises. You may think you're uptight about your boss when really you're mad at yourself for a mistake you made that he doesn't even know about. You may think you're mad at your spouse when really you're disappointed that you can't afford a new car. You may be irritated at a coworker because you regard her or him as a goof-off when really you're unconsciously envious of the good work she or he does. Tension is always present when something is undergoing change.

Handling tension is never easy. Don't expect it to be. When you feel yourself getting uptight under heavy stress, persuade yourself to relax. *Make your shoulders drop,* because they always seem to hunch up toward the neck when you're under pressure. Search inward for the *real cause* of the tension. Which disguise is covering up the culprit? Get away from your desk and office, if only for a few minutes. Tell yourself to cool it.

Allowing tension to take hold of you is a waste of your time. It slows you down, hampers you. When you feel its insidious grip, go limp and foil it. Caution yourself: *No one who is uptight all the time ever wins.* Tension is for losers.

Anxiety is the strangest of all our illnesses. And it is an illness because it can cause so much physical trouble for us. Anxiety is not fear. Fear is caused by a very real situation; when that situation is cleared up the fear disappears. But anxiety has no real situation as its base. *It is all a created monster in our minds.*

How do *you* cope with anxiety? How have you *been* coping? It seems that we have anxiety with us in some form from early childhood. Its root form is that we are anxious that we won't get something we want. Or that we'll get something we don't want, like an illness, a fall on the sidewalk, a holdup gun in our stomach, a flat tire on a lonely road, an air crash while we're flying. The list is endless.

Most adult anxiety has its roots in the unconscious conviction that we won't succeed in something when we want very much to succeed. We are, in effect, cutting our own confidence to ribbons, doubting our ability to be successful at something.

This self-doubt puts the hot air into most anxiety balloons. We become certain that we're not as good as we would like to be, that others are always better. We feel we have a better chance to fail than to win out. We find things we don't like about ourselves, and this starts a rash of inner conflicts. No one else knows about these conflicts, but everything we do is colored by them. They breed a hard sort of frustration because it is so difficult to *deal* with oneself. The frustration hangs on for a long time, and the self-doubt that plagues us fills a flock of anxiety balloons. Again, how do *you* cope with anxiety?

The next time you catch yourself feeling anxious, stop right there. Say to yourself, or say it aloud if you're alone: "This is ridiculous. I'm just going out of my way to make trouble for myself. There is no reason whatsoever for this feeling of anxiety. I'm just making it up, *so I'll unmake it right now.*"

You might memorize these little thoughts to use as pins to puncture those hot-air balloons of anxiety:

1. *Everyone* worries about whether he or she will measure up to the job ahead.

2. *Everyone* feels that most of the other people around are either a little bit better off or a great deal better off than he or she is.

3. *Everyone* goes to work each day wondering if his or her job is really safe.

4. *Everyone* is troubled with one form of anxiety or another, because few of us are all that sure that we are good enough to succeed.

Anxieties will never leave you alone. You'll have some of them all your life. But you can diminish their nasty effect on you by understanding that they are whipped up in the unconscious part of your mind, that they don't represent a real part of life.

Repeat: You can deal with fear because once the source of the actual fear is removed you no longer feel that emotion.

Repeat: Anxiety is a troubled seed that you plant yourself and water and fertilize with your imagination until it is large enough to wrap itself around you in an eternal grip.

Why hurt yourself?

A checklist for your good management emotions

Management emotions? Sure. What makes you think managers don't use their *good* emotions to manage and subdue their *bad* ones to keep out of trouble?

Here is a checklist of how managers use good emotions to open up their path to an executive position:

1. I'm eager to learn everything I can about this business because I find it exciting and highly interesting.

2. I won't make the mistake others do of becoming continually frustrated; frustration isn't reality, it is an emotion I've manufactured.

3. I know who I am. I don't have an identity crisis. I know my good points and my bad ones, and I'm making the best use of my good points.

4. If I occasionally become depressed I'll remember that a business-caused depression of my mind will usually go away in a few days, even a few hours.

5. I know that my confidence in myself is my greatest asset. It prevents me from feeling inferior to others and anxious about my job. I can do better work and make greater progress by confidence than by any other means.

6. I admire the decision-making process of management because it calls for the best I have in me. Making decisions is what I'm being paid to do.

7. I want success, but I'm reasonable about how I go about it. I've seen highly competitive people fall apart because they took everything so seriously and blew up many things out of proportion to reality.

8. I will make progress, but as I do I know I'll take on more responsibility. I won't let this additional responsibility break me down with tension, stress, anxiety. I anticipate more problem-solving tasks, and I'm ready for the challenge.

9. The persons who run this company are looking for new ideas and competent suggestions. I'll speak up and make myself heard whenever I have something substantial to pass on to them, even if it is in opposition to something they seem to be in favor of.

10. No one is in charge of my life except me. I will not be one of those persons who feel that, somehow, everything is going to work out all right for them. I'll plan my own life and work hard to get to where I feel I'm entitled to be because of my experience and ambition.

11. I won't wait for someone to tap me on the shoulder and say, "You're promoted!" I'll make my own breaks by being ready for the opportunities as they come. Being ready means I can anticipate what opportunities might open up and prepare myself with the kind of experience and background needed to fill the new job.

12. I have only so much time each day, and I'll use it as I spend money—carefully and for the best results. Wasting my time is wasting my opportunities to move ahead.

13. I'll have the human failing of inertia from time to time, but I'll overcome it by telling myself not to be smug and complacent but to stay in there and work harder.

14. I won't make the mistake of working just on the tasks that please me; I'll tackle the jobs that need to be done to promote my company.

15. I'll be an innovator, knowing that change is always with us and that there are always new and better ways to do things.

16. I have initiative and I'll use it to get things done. My company wants someone who can move the work, and I seek creative ways of getting the work done quickly, competently, effectively, and in line with my boss's goals.

17. Every morning when I come to work I'll tell myself that here is a bright new chance to make myself look good by doing good work.

18. I've seen rigid persons defeat themselves, and I know that to succeed I must remain flexible, must be able to adapt to new situations, new people, new places, new demands on me.

19. I don't regard anyone else as better than I am; they may be more experienced in some areas and have one or two things going for them, but I still feel that I'm as capable as anyone working for this corporation.

20. I know I can't do everything myself, that the true job of a manager is to get other people to do their share of the work. That, after all, *is* the art of management.

21. But I'm not misled by "managing," because I know that I must do a good share of the work myself. I know some people feel that "managing others" means they don't have to do any work themselves. Not me.

22. I feel that success is "energy used effectively."

23. I have a daily work plan, because I know that if I don't have a specific plan I'll be easily pulled away by distractions and diverted by them so that the major work goes unattended.

24. I'm sharply aware of some of the pitfalls I've seen others drop into, such as being overaggressive, not communicating properly to the employees above and the employees below, being conceited, acting arrogantly, and driving subordinates too hard.

25. I know there is no soft way to get to the top, that I must make it by proving myself, by working hard, by planning well, and by earning the right to become an executive.

Good emotions can't be bought. They can't be turned on like a shower faucet. They require years of unceasing effort to develop and keep in repair. Never a day goes by but that some assault isn't made by some person or some event on your good emotions. Under some attacks they can evaporate completely.

Your good management emotions are one of your finest tools. You can never afford to relax in your efforts to keep them strong. The best way to keep them strong is to use them each day. Like muscles, they become tougher and more productive for you through constant use. What happens to people when their muscles get soft?

A mental scissors to cut those "puppet strings"

"This is the way I've always been," a friend told me one day, "and I guess it's the way I'll always be."

He was in trouble again for a ridiculous characteristic—being late for work. "I've never known why being late is so much a part of my life-style," he went on. "It's always been that way, back as far as I can remember."

And it had caused him minor problems with every job he'd ever had. He was late meeting his wife, his friends, and his children. He was late for church, late for nearly everything.

The more he talked the more I knew he was being manipulated by "puppet strings" stretching back into childhood days. The real source was pushed out of his conscious and into his unconscious self. Where had this silly situation started?

Quite probably with a grade school teacher whom he disliked. Being so young and inexperienced, and dreading his entry into that particular classroom, he lagged behind at the school bell. He learned he could irritate *her* by being late. It was a weapon he could use to battle someone bigger than he.

As he grew older, the "puppet strings" still moved him. He'd forgotten about the teacher and his anxieties about facing her.

But his unconscious kept the emotion alive, and he was still responding mindlessly to it in his late thirties.

I've known many men and women who allow these childhood puppet strings to make them do things they should be mature enough not to do. The classic cases are the unconscious revolt against the father figure—anyone in authority who arouses childhood anxieties stemming from clashes with father; the neurotically competitive person who still is competing (unconsciously) against a brother or sister even though the brother or sister is many states away and sometimes long dead and buried; the fear against getting up and speaking in public because of a bad case of stage fright in elementary school, the effects of which were never overcome.

There are many different types of nearly invisible puppet strings pulling at us from the distant past. I have mine, some of which I've been able to see because I sought long and hard to find them. You have yours. When you find yourself acting in the same ineffective way, over and over again, as if you were a child instead of an adult, stop and make yourself think. *Where* are the strings attached, and how far back into childhood do they go? You will discover memory evidence that the strings exist.

More important, take a pair of mental scissors and cut yourself free of them. It can be done. All it takes is determination on your part to stop being manipulated by emotions that are tied to events and people of long ago.

Two ways to prove the world doesn't revolve around you

We're all a bit self-centered. And we have to fight against self-centeredness like mad. Being self-centered gives us a certain determination to get things for ourselves, to have our own way, to master our domain. But it also can make us come on pretty strong, to the point where we being to think the world revolves around us.

Here are some thoughts with which to prove to yourself that the world, in fact, does not revolve around you:

1. On the face of this earth there are billions of people. In the United States there are more than 210 million persons; about 54 million of them are men working for a living. What percentage of the male business population or female business population are you?

2. When was the last time you did anything that affected the *world?* If you are so important, what have you done that has changed anything drastically, started a new trend, shaken up the establishment?

Do you still feel that the world revolves around you?

How do you look to your family?

Mothers and fathers generally are forgiving, willing to make allowances, somewhat more able to comfort and console.

Your spouse and children see you differently. Knowing how you appear to *them* is extremely important to your well-being and to your ability to control your own destiny.

One of the tragic side effects of modern-day business is that it requires an extra amount of your own time to move ahead. You bring work home in your briefcase or stay later at the office. You travel and you're away from home. You can't be in two places at the same time, so in a way the family gets shortchanged.

When you do have some time, there's golf, bowling, skiing, working on the house, whatever. The days are endlessly filled with things to do, with small and large responsibilities.

Whether or not your spouse and children are forgiving, willing to make allowances, to comfort and console you is directly related to how much time you are able to spend with them, both in a group and individually. How well do you listen to them, help them with their problems? How often are you there when they need you?

I think one of the most acute problems for managers-becoming-executives is that you, for instance, can get so wrapped up in the chase after the big promotion that you neglect your family. You don't *think* you're neglecting them, because you are busy, with many important things to do. "Sometime soon" you will spend some time with the spouse and kids. Your intentions are good, but time goes on and you never really fulfill these pledges.

So you're in trouble with your own family. *First,* they don't see you as you see yourself. *Second,* while they have some empathy and understanding, they do have their own lives and problems and you often come second in importance to these. *Third,* despite your ambitions and hard work, they subjectively feel that you could do your job and *still* be home more often *to help them* with their problems and to be with them for things like picnics, going to the movies, eating out, short vacation trips, and working on special family projects.

There is a *fourth* element which has severely hurt the feelings of a lot of fine individuals who were caught in this failure to see how they looked to their family. *Rebellion.* Some sons and daughters have decided that the way their parents make a buck isn't for them. The old man has sold out for the gold, Mom's a slave to the establishment. They don't care about their own family, they'd sell their soul to get a big promotion. The rebellion works itself into fast and careless driving, the drug scene, sexual promiscuity, the wine and beer crowd, and senseless vandalism acts against schools, churches, public places.

Many hard-driving managers have come home to learn that one of their brood is in trouble. Others have found that their spouses couldn't care less about the big promotion or "what the boss said to me today."

Spend a little time guessing how *you* look to the family. If you're candid, you might not like what you see. The lesson is: *The job at home is as important as the job at the office.* Forget *that* lesson and you'll end up in trouble more searing than any you could get into at the office.

Why you do the things you do

Done anything kooky lately? Done anything that you regretted immediately? Done anything that made you wonder how in the world you did it in the first place because "it isn't me at all!"?

Emotions, hidden deep within you, make you do some oddball things at times. Frustration and boredom are the biggest factors triggering unusual and impromptu behavior.

One executive got into a shouting match with a waiter because he forgot to bring him cream for his coffee.

Another savagely kicked a vending machine that took her money and didn't give her a pack of cigarettes.

Another furtively packed the bath towels from a motel room when he left.

Another made a suggestive remark to a young salesperson.

Another stayed downtown one night and hung one on even though he hadn't had a drink in months and could suggest no real reason to have the first one on that particular night.

There's a bit of Weird Harold in all of us. It comes out in the transference mechanism. We're upset about one thing and take out our frustration on another. Unconsciously we say, "I've been hurt, so *somebody* is going to pay!" We find some way, usually without any forethought, to make somebody or something pay for our frustration or boredom.

If you're starting to do more than a few kooky things lately, you'd better look to the basic reason. You're frustrated somewhere. But where?

What sort of an aggression level do you have?

Top management is fond of saying that it looks for "aggressive managers."

"To be aggressive" means "to make attacks." In the business world this aggressiveness is supposed to be used in tackling problems, in learning new ways, in meeting sales and production quotas, in doing everything possible to keep the company growing and prospering . . . and paying good dividends.

Aggressiveness is not a native characteristic with every person. Is it with you? Let's take a look at your aggression level:

1. You never worry about meeting new people.
2. You never worry about going into a meeting where you're on the agenda to give a talk or make a report.
3. You never worry about going in to talk to a top executive about a big idea you've thought out and are ready to present to him or her.
4. You aren't too concerned when things go wrong because you see areas where the damage can be easily repaired and a small defeat turned into a nice victory.
5. You have your eye on a job above you and you're convinced that you'll be chosen to fill it when the time comes.

Worry? Who, me?

Of course you worry. You worry so much at times that you tremble a bit, feel a sour stomach coming, wish you were somewhere else. That's *normal*.

Your aggression level is high if you can *overcome* your anxiety at any particular time *and go on and do the job properly*.

Don't kid yourself that the seemingly "aggressive managers" aren't filled with doubt, anxiety, trepidation. They've just learned to control these nagging emotions because they know that the only way they can get things done is to *attack* the immediate problem.

To attack problems is to be aggressive. It works. You've seen it work for others. It will work for you.

The point: No matter how much you're worried about a particular task you must do and want to do, *there is nothing to keep you from doing it except your lack of aggressiveness*.

If you don't try, you've just caved in to your bad emotions. You've given yourself a weak excuse such as, "They won't listen to me," or "It didn't work for someone else, it won't work for me," or "Why beat your head against a stone wall?" Excuses may make you feel a little bit better, but they don't help you get the job done. And if you don't consistently improve in getting jobs done you're not going very far up the management ladder into the executive suite.

Knowing your affinity for leadership

Leading other people can be a pain in the neck. But it is an essential part of your management armament. I mean armament in the traditional way. You strap a sort of a leadership sword around your waist each day. It serves, by virtue of being in sight, to persuade some of your subordinates to pay attention to you. It serves, when you pull it out and swing it around, to convince others that you mean what you say and have the power to back it up.

You don't "lead" people. The term is ridiculous, although in management jargon it is used all the time. You either persuade them or you force them.

If you feel that people will "follow" you because you're a swell person, because you're right, because you're more capable than they are, you're standing on the wrong foot. Subordinates help you create the illusion that you are the leader because they fear your ability to fire them, to not give them a pay raise, to make their life unpleasant, or because they seek to use you and your power to further their own interest. It is a game but a serious one for all of you.

Your affinity for leadership is directly related to your knowledge of how the leadership system works.

How would you answer these statements—yes or no?

1. Very few people who work for me will eagerly help me win a promotion.

2. The ones who work the hardest for me are the ones who most want something for themselves.

3. They accept me as their "leader" only as long as I have the power to reward them or punish them.

4. They will quickly transfer their allegiance to anyone who might replace me or be able to push me out of the way.

5. I can keep them interested in helping me achieve the goals my company wants me to gain only as long as I persuade them that *their* best interests are served as well.

6. While we work together, they don't owe me anything because fortune has placed them under my "leadership," and I don't owe them anything special either, other than normal courtesy, consideration, and attention.

7. We all will work effectively together as a unit only to the extent that we all feel we're going to get something from this mutual effort.

If you said "yes" to these statements you've got the hang of it. Leadership isn't granted, it's negotiated—day after day, week after week.

What have you done to help yourself?

You're smart enough not to expect everything good to happen to you because of other people. Other people ordinarily don't go out of their way to do "good things" for you. Often the best thing they can do is *not* to do something *bad* for you. You help yourself best when you do most of it yourself.

What have you done lately to help yourself?

How about some of these activities?

1. Discussed management problems with older managers in other companies so that you gain their insight on how to handle yourself and your subordinates?

2. Read a good book or two on the psychology of management?

3. Attended a seminar or lecture on management?

4. Read one or more of the periodicals on management?

5. Gone off by yourself for an hour or so of solitude to think

about the realities of life, how much more you need to work with yourself to cope with greater responsibilities as you move up, how you'll fight to avoid drifting along and to work to control your own destiny by planning ahead and deciding where you want to go and who you want to be?

Try some of these, or all of them, and you're boosting yourself right along.

Deciding where you need improvement

You're not perfect. No one is. You need to work constantly at improving yourself. You *are* unique. No one else in the world is exactly like you. But you're human, and there are areas in which you need to strengthen your human qualities and your management muscles. With an eye on the previous pages of this chapter, let's review some of them:

1. I need to develop a stronger attitude toward success. I want it to show through so that when they're with me my subordinates and my bosses feel a sort of atmosphere of success surrounding me. I know that I will be only what I *believe* myself to be, and I will *believe* that I am a person equipped with the positive attitude toward success.

2. I'm more or less the center of attention at the office, with everything I do visible to my subordinates and bosses. Since I am clearly visible, I will make the most of this opportunity to show the others that I am a capable, dependable, talented manager who is developing into a prospective executive. Since I have an audience I'll play it like a professional.

3. I won't cut myself to pieces because I've compared myself to someone I feel is more successful or more talented than I am. Why agonize myself this way? I know it's often an illusion that the others *are* more successful or more talented. I will refuse to take on any more of this kind of self-inflicted worry. I'll concen-

trate on making myself more attractive to promotion, not on making invidious comparisons with others.

4. I'll remind myself each day that troubles are part of the game. I can't strengthen myself to become a top executive unless I build my emotional muscles to deal with everyday problems. I'll accept them as normal events and not take them as personal affronts.

5. I can't make a giant leap into the executive suite. I have to earn my way into it. I can do this best by *planning my way*, by breaking down my goals into fairly easily attainable objectives. I'll use my ambitions, my restless desires, to develop the effective kind of work habits that will allow me to achieve these objectives.

6. I know that emotions are locked into my every action. I'll work relentlessly at understanding *why* I feel and act the way I do, and why *others* act and feel the way they do. I'm dealing with complicated human beings, and I'll not take for granted that my recognition by them as a person of merit and distinction is absolutely assured. I'll work constantly to earn it; I'll knock my self-doubt on the head and stifle my anxieties.

7. I'll keep an eye on the overall picture of my corporation. I know that I'm "part of the team," that top management *wants* managers like me to move up and bring with me my ideas, suggestions, talents, strengths, and capabilities to help them reach their goals. I'll stay loose, as opposed to being rigid, and this flexibility will help me be a more enthusiastic part of the team—an achiever, not a critic.

8. By understanding more of the mechanics of the corporation, I can line up my personal goals more effectively with those of top management. I'll participate in the decision-making process to the extent that I can show top management I'm qualified, so I'll work on being qualified. I'll refuse to "play it safe," and I'll express myself honestly whenever I feel I have something of substance to say. I'll catch top management's eye only when I

seize the appropriate opportunities to make myself heard ... and visible.

9. I'll work both at understanding myself and at having empathy and sympathy for others. We're all in this together and need one another, and if we get along well we'll all succeed to some degree. I'll succeed the most because *I want to* and because *I'm earning the right to success.*

These are some of the areas where you need improvement in your outlook. There are many more, naturally, but these are among the most important ones.

So you think you know who you are?

You'll never, during your entire life, know yourself perfectly. But when you work at freeing yourself from some of the emotional handcuffs and at developing a better liking for both yourself and others you clear the way for you to become far more successful.

Success? It's relative—but why labor in middle management when you can reach the top? Why stay in the $10,000 to $20,000 bracket when you can move up to $30,000 to $40,000 and higher?

Why, indeed?

CHAPTER THREE

Why No One Can Keep You from the Top . . . but You

How recently have you caught yourself reading the employment ads in *The Wall Street Journal?* How recently have you gotten out the old résumé and dusted it off to mail it in response to an ad in the Sunday business section of your local newspaper? How long has it been since you mentioned to a close friend, "Keep an ear open for something for me, will you?"

These are some of the symptoms of a manager who feels his or her way to the top of the corporation is blocked.

If your dissatisfaction is such that you have recently done one or all of these, then it's time for you to look at that dissatisfaction carefully and find out what *really* is the problem.

First, take apart your dissatisfaction and examine it

Why do you want to make a move? What are the things that have happened to disenchant you with your present position? Are these among the reasons?

1. No pay raise for a long period of time.
2. Promotion of someone you regard as inferior to you.
3. Changes in top management and you're not lined up with the newcomers.
4. You are playing a decreasingly important role in the decision-making process.
5. You've developed a case of "wrong chemistry" between yourself and someone in authority.
6. Your workload is "enormous" and you don't have enough help.
7. Your immediate superior has been trying to take credit for the good work you have done.
8. You've come to the conclusion that you don't like the people at the office with whom you work.
9. You're convinced that if you open your mouth to present constructive criticism someone at the top whom you don't like will seize the opportunity to chop off your head. "You can't beat city hall."
10. You feel you're not with the "in crowd" who run the company, that in a sense you've been rejected. "Only the promoters can make it into the crowd in this company."

All right. *Why do you feel blocked?* Why do you feel frustrated? Why are you experiencing anxiety and depression? Why do you feel you must make a move to another company? What are you trying to escape from?

Quite likely the trouble is one or more of the tension builders I've listed above. *But should you make a move?* Read the following statements; then put this book down for a few minutes and *think* about what they mean to you:

1. You accepted your present position, probably with enthusiasm. What were the incentives that made you take your present job?

2. If you quit and move elsewhere, there are chances that you can't make it any further in the new company than you did right where you are. You take yourself right along, and you might find the exact same conditions waiting for you at the new place. How do you know?

3. Are you certain that you have *solid reasons* for leaving, or might it be that you've allowed your bad emotions to control you?

In perfect truth if you *are* completely blocked, then it is wise to move as quickly as you can. Before you move, you will try to ascertain that your new job will give you more promise for advancement than your old one.

Many managers have thought of themselves as "blocked" and moved out to work elsewhere. In many cases they left the next promotion to other people who didn't really deserve them. They failed to talk to their boss and fully determine what their future was with their company. They "moved along" and lost promotions that could have been theirs but for *their self-inflicted frustration.*

Do you have to move? Why can't you take your dissatisfaction and put it to work for you right where you are? Have you thought of that? Your goal is to reach the executive suite. You can do it right in the company where you presently work. Why not?

Let's go on and take a look at how you can do this, despite any uneasiness you now feel, any bitterness about how you feel you're being treated unfairly, any anxiety about your job being in jeopardy, or any depression that has seeped into you along with the sick feeling that the deck is stacked against you. I'm going to convince you that no one can keep you from the top—except you.

Second, let's explore the type of people who are at the top

These individuals could be *you* because they were much like you when they were your age. They were ambitious and wanted more out of life than just a job. Now they're at the top, and they have the power to make or break you.

The best kind of top executives are not totally self-centered; they have room to be courteous, considerate, helpful. These are the people who genuinely want those younger than them to move up and be trained to one day take over some of the top-management functions. They don't necessarily go out of their way to boost young managers, because they are busy and they may be intruding into someone else's territory. But they help when they can. They also can provide excellent advice on what to do and how to get there. These are the executives with strength and courage and farsightedness. They know they are helping their company when they help up-and-coming managers.

The mediocre kind of top executives got where they are by outlasting or outliving everyone else in competition, or they had family friends plugging for them. It is always a mystery *why* these executives got where they are and why they *remain*. You can expect very little compassion and understanding from this type of person. They're holding on to what they have. They're not interested in helping anyone move up from below. They'll smile at you and listen to you, but they'll seldom do anything to help you achieve a promotion. They may be tempted to take credit for what you and others do. Yes, they are usually that kind.

The worst kind of top executives feel best when everyone else is kept in the dark. The less anyone knows about what they're doing the safer they feel. They couldn't care less about anyone else in the organization. Everything they do is angled to put them in a good light or to shove someone else into a bad light. They want as much power as they can seize because if they have it then it can't be used against them. Protecting *themselves* is what their game plan is all about. How much fair treatment can you expect from *these* people?

How concerned is top management with the struggling managers below them? It depends, as you've seen from the three classifications I've drawn above. The better top executives are often acutely concerned for one or more managers and actively work to help them up the ladder. Despite their strenuous schedules they take the time to evaluate managers who have caught their eye and to recommend them for promotion or for a series of assignments which will further develop them to a point where they can merit a promotion. They know that developing managers into executives is an important part of their responsibilities. Top executives are very much concerned with developing good people from within.

The prevalent feeling among the worst top executives is: "The managers have jobs, they have profit sharing, health plans, all that, so let *them* worry about getting to the top."

When *you're* at the top, *you'll* take the time to give more than lip service to the "little people." I know one manager who, when the top of his company suddenly collapsed and he had a chance to become executive vice president, shouted: "Now the little people around here will be heard!" As time went on it became clear that he menat *himself*. He was no different from the previous "worst" executives and did not last long in his unfamiliar role as executive vice president.

When you do make it you'll not feel that your only *major* goal is to *stay* up there. You'll work hard and you'll help others. There will be many times when you will do something to help an aspiring manager move up the ladder. Even if he's moving on what seems to be a collision course toward *your* job!

Third, what do the people at the top want from you?

Almost without exception the qualities which they want *you* to possess and which they search for in your record include these:

1. *Dependability*. A person they can depend on to get any job done, a simple one or a tough one.

2. *Professionalism*. Doing your own job of acquiring information from specific sources, taking the size of the problem and finding a description for it, figuring out several methods by which the problem can be handled, selecting the method that seems to be the best, doing what needs to be done to solve the problem, and reporting briefly to your superior. In short, distinct signs of professional organization of yourself.

3. *Enthusiasm*. They need your enthusiasm, which can rub off on them. They note this attitude and score it highly. Anyone they tag as a comer must be able to express his enthusiastic interest in tackling increasingly tougher assignments. They know an unenthusiastic manager is often a poor bet to get the job done the way they want it handled.

4. *Curiousness*. Not nosiness, curiousness. Which means that you are interested in learning many new things and are always asking questions, reading new publications and books, finding out what other people are doing and why. Top management executives know that this type of curiosity is preparing a manager to take on greater responsibilities. They know that he or she is flexible, a learner, and not rigid.

5. *Decisiveness*. Many a manager had ended up in Nowheresville because he or she couldn't make good decisions and make them fast enough. The ability to make decisions is tantamount to leadership, and that is one of the things top management is looking for in you. They don't care so much if your decision is occasionally wrong as they do that you make a strong decision at the appropriate time and stick with it.

6. *Determination*. There are too many half-hearted managers in this world. A manager who is determined to get to the top, who is determined to acquire the skills she or he needs, will draw more than passing attention from those at the top. A determined individual will make decisions and get things done. *That's* what they want.

7. *Harmony.* This is your ability to work harmoniously with even the greatest S.O.B. in the world or the dumbest kook in the world. It means working in harmony with individuals or groups when there are sharp edges, booby traps, and pitfalls to endanger you. It means you have to give up something, such as your temper, in order to achieve results in harmonious endeavors! But it's one of the things they demand from you.

8. *People-orientation.* Few managers get things done all by themselves. They must encourage, persuade, motivate, or force other people, their subordinates, to do most of the work. Managers who upstage or downgrade their subordinates or create disharmony between themselves and their subordinates are going nowhere. You, on your way up, understand what being "people-oriented" means to you. It means handling your people effectively to get the work done.

These are among the things top management *wants* from you.

How about the things they will *give* to you?

Fourth, what will the people at the top GIVE to you?

It's amazing how much help you can get from the people at the top if you discard some illusions and forget some myths about top management and if you take these positive attitudes:

1. I *can* talk to the people at the top without fear of losing my job or causing trouble for myself if I start out well prepared and certain of my facts.

2. None of those in top management are all that assured that everything they're doing is success-bound. Good executives want ideas and suggestions to help them and competent support for their workable programs. I can give these individuals facts and figures to aid in their analysis of the various situations that affect them.

3. I know that top executives as a group worry most about these problems:

- Profits for shareholders
- Borrowing money and being a good credit risk
- Price increases or price cuts
- Inroads in their sales areas by competitors
- Closing down unprofitable operations
- Acquiring new and profitable operations
- Government action that might hamper progress
- Marketing
- Getting "good people"

With these problems come the ready-made opportunities for me to give them the data and facts which they can use in making decisions that affect the company.

What can executives *give* me? Opportunities to make myself visible to them, to make myself part of their working activities. Opportunities to prove that I am dependable, a business-minded manager who knows the score and can be a mainstay in their individual and group activities.

I know that half the battle is *seeing* the opportunities that exist to make myself more valuable to top management. The other half is taking advantage of those opportunities.

Fifth, how do you measure up to top management's requirements?

Top management is willing to trade with you. They'll trade bits of their authority for some of your energetic pursuit of problem-solving programs. Measuring up to their requirements, which we looked at a few pages ago, includes the following:

1. Knowing exactly what the parameters of my corporate environment are. What are the outer limits of my specific responsibilities? Am I measuring up to the full limits of my job? Am I doing everything they want me to do, in the manner they prefer? Where could I overstep my bounds and encroach on someone else's territory?

2. Knowing the critical needs of my boss and where his (or her) greatest interests lie. By studying his style of operation I can find ways to help him achieve his objectives instead of hinder.

3. Knowing that much of day-to-day management is "body contact." I must meet my boss and other top executives eyeball to eyeball and be objective about the many problems facing us. I can't afford to take a single thing in a personal sense because it is seldom meant that way. I won't fade into a yes-man, but I will present the facts as I see them clearly and intellectually.

4. Knowing that I am being paid to be a disciplined subordinate to my boss and an expert assistant to the other top executives. They need my skills and talents. They need my personal judgment to add another dimension to the effective management of this corporation. I will bring to them my assessment of the negative and positive aspects of each problem.

5. Knowing that the art of communication with my boss and other top executives is essential to my growth in the corporation. The more I establish good two-way communication, the more I can develop myself as an executive-in-training. I'll learn new concepts, new methods, new work habits, new depths of understanding.

Measuring up to the requirements that top management has set for you isn't all that difficult. To get anywhere in this world you have to meet *someone's* requirements. By being aware of what top management wants of you, you can work toward meeting the requirements. Every time you do strengthen yourself in your push upward toward an executive job of your own.

Sixth, do you really understand the concept of the corporation?

Just because a business organization *exists* doesn't mean it shouldn't be understood. Let me ask you this question: What makes it work?

Today's huge corporation has plenty of real estate, brick and mortar, products, distribution facilities, sales outlets, people, income, expenses, dividends, organizational charts, job descriptions, responsibilities, legalities, tons of paper forms, and a name. But what makes it *function?* Where is the heart of the corporation? The chairperson of the board? The president and chief executive officer? The top-management group? Where?

This question is almost unanswerable. We know that a modern corporation (or a lesser business, as well) has these elements:

1. Its purpose is to make money for its owners.

2. It uses the skills and talents of a great many different types of people.

3. It organizes these people into a bureaucratic system designed to help it make money and stay in business.

4. Because it holds so many people together it can offer substantial benefits such as paid vacations, savings plans, hospital and medical insurance, profit sharing plans, bonuses, retirement plans, pension systems, and other forms of security benefits, plus the opportunity for an individual to meet many other people.

5. It offers steady work to its people so that they can plan ahead for their own advantage. It offers consistent work responsibilities with well-spaced-out changes designed to be fairly digestible over a period of time. In short, no series of great shocks each day. Usually!

6. It provides *you* with an opportunity to grab some security while you work hard to elevate yourself to the top, where the rewards, and prestige, are greater.

The *large corporation* of today is complex, highly technological, beset with many exterior problems such as pollution control and the need to protect the environment while it still is struggling to perfect and lubricate its interior organization. Its problems are massive and unending. More than in the past it faces critics of its financial efforts and payouts, of its social participation, of the reliability and serviceability of its products, and of the conduct of its officers. But it has arrived, it is on The New York Stock

Exchange, is one of *Fortune*'s 500, and has much muscle and power to hold its position.

The *medium corporation* may find itself stunted because it is in a product or service area where its growth is restricted by natural forces. If its management also lacks the initiative to get outside funding and to acquire new product lines to expand it may well stagnate in one spot for years. Depending on its situation, it may be on the Big Board, the American Stock Exchange, or one of the small exchanges, or its stock may be sold over-the-counter. Its major problem is that of preventing a larger corporation or a more competitive medium-sized corporation from entering its field and taking its marbles. It also tends to lose its agressiveness when its management plays safe.

The *small corporation* may be a lot of fun because many of its managers and executives are gung ho about the future and their prospects of "making it big." They feel that there is no way to go but up and they're the team that can do it. The problems are serious; they may be gobbled up by a large corporation, they may become overextended financially and become prey to competitors, they may back a few wrong adventures and lose too much cash and income. They also may lose many of their best people to medium and large corporations, so that there always is a problem of maintaining a consistent staff level.

The *small business*—industrial, retail, service, what have you—appeals to a lot of managers. It's the "big-fish-in-the-small-pond" syndrome. But small businesses come and go with alarming regularity, and the type of security they offer sometimes is questionable. Their biggest problems are those of financing and long-range planning.

The *"family business"* is one of the toughest nuts for managers and executives to crack. The family maintains a death grip on the business for as long as it can. The most serious problem is that of aged family members still "coming down to the office every day" and negating all progressive and aggressive plans and programs. Getting caught between feuding members of "the family" can be the worst situation in your life. Though there are some opportunities in this type of concern, the odds are that you'll never get far unless you become a family pet—and what kind of an executive are you then?

The *other business organizations* include banks, insurance companies, automotive dealerships, real estate firms, agricultural firms, food service companies, household goods moving firms, retail stores of all sizes and types, restaurants, very small manufacturing firms, and hundreds of other groups of from 2 to 100 persons. America has hundreds of thousands of small businesses, and they provide a good living to many people. Their only drawback is the limit to how far you can go. Many a person has made it to the top starting in a small branch office, or a franchise operation, and moving into corporate headquarters later on.

But in all these, *your* assignment is to understand how *your* company is organized, how it got started, what its history has been, *why* it is structured the way it is today, where it wants to go, and what its current problems are.

Your challenge is to find ways in which you can help that business grow and prosper—and stay in business. You can't take it for granted that you "know all about" the company. Study it, research it, ask questions, read background material, do a bit of sleuthing. If *this* is the structure that's going to carry your weight to the top, you'd better find out how sturdy and dependable it is.

Seventh, look at the changes taking place in United States business

We're fond of saying, "Things are changing so fast I can't keep up." Coping with change is a large part of your life-style as a manager in training to be an executive. Changes are going on in these areas all the time:

1. People's preferences for products
2. People's preferences for services

3. The way people save or spend money

4. The way people regard business, politics, the economy, national security, taxes, government spending, clothing styles, food and beverage preferences, leisure-time activities, social life, the environment, natural resources, and working for a living

5. Employee's sensitivities toward managers and executives, the environment in which they work, and the conditions under which they work

6. Unions versus management politics

7. Shareholder attitudes toward corporate management

8. Individuals, who are constantly shifting their personal likes and dislikes to accommodate the emotional patterns in themselves and their families, patterns that ride up and down with the currents of the times

Change is part of your problem. Look at what has happened in the last five, ten, and twenty years. Incredible changes have occurred in the way we Americans act and think. It takes no special skill to look ahead and predict that more incredible changes are on the way.

Few of us can predict accurately what these changes will be. The main thing as far as you are concerned is for you to be "change-oriented," flexible enough to accept the beginnings of change and adaptable enough *to change yourself* when need be. Keeping up with changes everywhere is part of your job.

You might even initiate a few changes of your own right there in your environment.

Lastly, where will you fit at the top?

Does your concept of "the top" include these elements?

1. The top is where I will have some power—power to protect my security, power to protect myself from others, power to be a bit more free from the pressing worries about failure.

2. The top is where I can rack up some significant achieve-

ments for my company. Not only can I achieve for myself but I can do some things I've always wanted to do for my company.

3. The top is where I can enjoy some of the goodies of life, club memberships, the company car, bigger expense accounts, more prestige, things like that.

4. The top is where I'll earn more recognition from my spouse and children, my relatives and friends. They'll be more aware of what a swell gal or guy I am because I've made it up to the top.

These are perfectly normal thoughts when you deal with a concept of the top. Few individuals would be willing to suffer the long trek up there and the intensely hard work patterns that propel them if they didn't perceive the rewards they'll get.

Power, money, prestige, self-satisfaction, attention-generating successes are powerful motivations for all of us.

Question 1: It is no crime to be ambitious and want to work your way into the executive suite. The question is, *which executive position do you want*? Say that you want to be vice president, sales. The duties change a bit from corporation to corporation, and so does the working environment, but generally the total burden of marketing falls on your shoulders. To fill *this* job, what background must you have? It isn't enough to have been a salesman out in the field for a few years. You need to know a great deal about marketing surveys, market analysis, advertising, publicity, promotion, and all the other facets of marketing. You need to know what your industry is doing and how your corporation compares to it; how your competitors are doing and how your corporation compares to them. In short, the scope of a vice president, sales, position is extremely broad. And it is an unending "painful-stomach" job because of the severe ups and downs, the sharp jolts and sudden shocks, that this area of livelihood can bring.

Or you want to be *vice president, manufacturing*. The technological advances of recent years and those in the offing right now make the production process extremely complicated. The general idea is to have computer- or tape-controlled machinery and "systems" do more work with fewer people. People need attention and are less reliable than machinery, or so many vice presidents in manufacturing think. Your concern is the brick and mortar of the production facilities, materials handling, raw materials acquisition and storage, warehousing, shipping, quality control, in-plant training, all that. The stress is somewhat less than that generated in sales but it is still there. The pressure is on you to produce more products at less cost by stepping up productivity, cutting expenses, making everything more efficient. You sometimes wonder if it can ever be done.

Or you want to be *general manager*. You have profit responsibility for your division or plant. You're kingpin there, but you report to a vice president. Many individuals find deep satisfaction in this arrangement. They are, in effect, president of their own "company within a company." It provides them with the personal success sensation they've been seeking.

Or you want to be *president*. No fooling around for you! Here is the biggest payoff, and here is the biggest set of headaches. You'll do very little of the hard day-to-day work, but you'll use your brain down to where you feel it needs frequent oiling. The competition for the president's office is intense. One office and so many seekers. You *must* qualify, and this very qualification prohibits *you* from wasting any more time and from *not* preparing yourself carefully to qualify.

Question 2: Now that you have your eye on a particular spot at the top, *do you know what kind of a person you must be to become a top executive?*

You won't be exactly the person you are today. There are both subtle and outright changes that will take place in you by the time you move into the executive suite.

Here is a sort of yardstick by which many top executives are measured:

1. They are extremely accomplished individuals who've spent their entire work lives sharpening their capabilities.

2. They possess enormous confidence in their specialized lines because they have spent so many years preparing themselves to handle the burdens of the office.

3. They beat someone else out here and there on their way up, a mark of their competitive sense and unwillingness to sit back and let someone else win the better jobs.

4. Yet, with all this, they have holes in their characters. Many of them become too self-important, assuming a godlike air that they can do no wrong. Some hit the bottle more than they should because the stress of staying at the top is enormous. Some try to escape the constant pressure by playing golf too much (yes, it can be done), having affairs, going too deeply into a hobby. There are plenty of normal top executives, but there are also some who got there because of several bad reasons and are fighting down their reputations.

5. The obsession with survival is all-enveloping at the top. At any given moment there is a subtle struggle for power going on in any executive suite. It may not be noticeable, but it is there. The executives know that the only ones who survive at the top are those who hold the power, such as large blocks of voting stock or the backing of outsiders who hold large chunks of stock. So power in any corporation comes down to money and influence. Was it ever any different in any element of American life?

6. Free-floating ability comes in those instances where the top executives have no hard and firm path to follow and go at it sort of willy-nilly. I've been amazed in my adulthood to realize how many corporations do not have really well-worked-out plans for the present or the future. Everything seems to be done under pressure and at the moment of expediency. Executives who can survive in this free-floating atmosphere have to have a special trait for the job.

7. Vanity, which may be considerable. Having made it to the top, most executives naturally want to witness some respect from their subordinates. Unfortunately, some top people want more attention than they deserve. Others take advantage of their positions to force their immediate team members to be sycophants, yes-men, supporters whose admiration seemingly never dims. I've known many fine people at the top who never indicated any

undue vanity, and I've known countless others who swam in the stuff.

8. Long service with the same corporation inevitably bows even the strongest back in the executive suite. My close friends in other companies who have experienced this tension building up inexorably over the years want to "retire early," wish they had "mixed up their career by working at various companies" instead of one, and feel that somehow they "did a disservice to myself" by remaining so long at one corporation. If *you* stay with the same company for twenty, thirty, or more years, you will experience the same inevitable build-up in pressure.

The picture of the "average top executive" is not clear. There is no hard-and-fast rule about who will make it to the top. We do know in surveying those who made it that they possessed some characteristics fairly common to them all. Ambition, drive, inexhaustible energy, powerful motivations, ability to learn new things, ability to change and shift courses when it was necessary, ability to tolerate others' opinions and actions, ability to solve problems on an objective basis.

Question 3: Are you ready to prepare yourself for a faster rise to the top?

Which of these areas needs your improvement?

- Understanding your emotions better
- Understanding more about how to motivate and control the work of other people
- Learning more about the financial part of your corporation
- Learning more about the production-distribution part
- Learning more about the shareholder-profit part
- Learning more about the data processing part
- Learning how to be more articulate, to put your points across verbally in meetings
- Learning how to be more concise and direct in written items, such as reports, memos, correspondence
- Learning how to chair committee meetings
- Learning more about the industry your corporation serves

72   Manager Today, Executive Tomorrow

- Learning more about your competitors
- Learning how to cope with your equals at the manager level (your competitors for the next promotion)
- Learning more about the social responsibilities of the corporation
- Learning more about protecting the environment, preserving natural resources, using fuel efficiently, using antipollution controls
- Learning more about labor-management cooperative actions
- Learning more about employee relations

The list is endless. Make up your *own list,* and see where you have work to do. But notice how I used the word "learning" over and over.

Question 4: Are you ready to work on your own emotion control? You're never without some emotions at any given moment. The way to look at emotions, as far as your successful growth toward the top is concerned, is *to replace bad emotions with good emotions.*

Since you feel an emotion, or several, why not put the good ones to work for you?

I've always said that the bad habit of smoking can be replaced with *the good habit of not smoking.* The questionable habit of drinking booze at every opportunity can be replaced with the more healthy habit of *not* drinking booze at every opportunity. Think about it.

Here are some of the *positive* ways of handling emotions. You can see how, if you concentrate on them, they'll relieve the pressure from a correspondingly bad emotion—*to your benefit.*

1. *Frustration* is not fact; it is merely a way to feel terrible without any clear reason to do so. When I begin to feel frustrated I remind myself that *I am the one who is hurting myself by imagining that I am in trouble.*

2. *Fearing failure* is a normal human emotion, but I can control it by reminding myself that I've *won* many times and have failed

very few times. Everyone fails now and then, because all of us are imperfect. But I will not allow my fear of failure to take me over and prevent me from working hard to succeed.

3. *Perfectionism* will only cause me trouble because I'm not perfect, nor is anyone else. I'll look for the satisfactory answer to the problem, for the satisfactory work level of my subordinates, for the satisfactory conclusion of any of my work programs.

4. *Pressure* comes in all sizes and forms, and from problems that pop up without warning. I'll avoid as much pressure as possible by reminding myself that none of the problems is personal, that I am capable of tolerating difficult problems and maintaining my cool.

5. *Conflict* is within me at every moment. I'm always at war with myself over some small thing. I understand this and control it, knowing that my maturity is to be relied on and my emotional tugging is to be put aside. I'll work toward making my objectivity far greater in strength than my subjectivity.

6. *Anxiety* is something else I can do without, because it is tied in with a frustrating conflict within me. I get to the point where I feel that I'm being blocked and can't do anything about it. Then anxiety sets in and follows me every moment of the day, for a very long time. I can prevent anxiety by reminding myself that it is another unreal emotion. There is no real reason for me to feel anxious. I know anxiety is one of humanity's worst mental diseases, and I'll fight hard to prevent it from seeping in on my mental process. I'll use this energy for better purposes.

7. *Hostility* is another bad trip. Who needs it? If I resent something someone has done, I do not have to feel hostility toward that person or about the incident. The emotion of hostility is a mental method of making things worse than they are. It means I'm overreacting to someone or am reacting to a situation far more than it is worth. Cooling hostility is a mark of maturity, and I'd rather be mature than mad all the time. It takes energy to be mad; why waste my energy?

8. *Reluctance to change* is bad news. Why should I be reluc-

tant to accept change when this world has always been changing? The worst thing I can do is to plug for status quo. I want change, to be part of an ever-opening world of new ideas, new concepts, new ways of doing things, new ways of looking at things, of newness. If I am reluctant to change, all I'll do is give myself a bad fit of anxiety, and why should I do that?

9. *Inferiority* is a word I've heard all my life. It means that if I don't believe I can succeed at my job, my marriage, whatever, then I'll feel inferior. It means I tell myself, "I can't make it!" It means I'm hurting myself again because I'm sopping with self-pity, I'm afraid I'll be fired, I worry about what other people will think and say about me, I can't forget some goofs I made at the office or some social blunders I pulled. It means I can't take the slightest criticism without going to pieces inside; or it means that when someone compliments me I overreact and practically walk on air. I know that feeling inferior means that unconsciously I am worried about handling my job, that I feel others at the office are better than I am and that my job is on the line. My sense of maturity tells me that feeling inferior is totally unnecessary because *I have not failed, I have not created a mess, and I am in fact on the way to the top.* Everyone has to fight feeling inferior from time to time. It's a holdover from when we were children. But as adults we don't need this residual immaturity. I'll kick it to one side.

10. *Confidence* is the antidote to the fears that bad emotions set up within me. I'll concentrate on developing more confidence by accepting myself, recognizing and minimizing my weaknesses, working toward my strengths. I will conduct myself in true sincerity, not be a stranger to myself, accept others for what they are, and control my emotions so that I can succeed to the extent I desire.

That's quite an order.

Now that you've done such serious thinking as this, spend a bit more time in solitude assessing your good and bad qualities. Take the view that here, now, at this very moment, there is a turning point for you. A turning point at which you move out of the managerial doldrums and start your push toward the top.

For the truth is: No matter what your age, or your position, or your work history, NOW is the time of crisis for you. NOW is the time you can begin to make your moves, moves which if done in a professional manner will take you to where you want to be in the business world. To an executive office at the top.

CHAPTER FOUR

Your Master Plan for Getting Yourself Going

Master plan? Do I *really* need one? Aren't they mostly wishful thinking? A lot of hard work done for nothing because of the capricious way things change so rapidly these days? Why should I put effort into a master plan?

Yes, you need one. No, they're not wishful thinking. If you don't prepare yourself with a clear mental road map, a definite blueprint, a calculated checklist for success, whatever you want to call it, you lessen your chances of getting to the top.

In my interviews with hundreds of executives I've come to doubt that anyone ever made it out of the managerial office and into the executive suite without some version of a predetermined game plan. Most of the individuals I talked to knew where they were going. Success is not happenstance. Success is the result of careful planning and carefully done work.

There may be some luck involved in being successful but not very much. The successful people I've worked with made it because they had the ambition, the energy, and their version of a master plan to get there. Some of them admitted candidly that they were not conscious that they had planned everything so well, but most of them revealed that they knew where they were going and how to get there. That's a master plan.

How to start your personal master plan

Here are some excellent tips offered by the persons who "made it."

You start first with an attitude, as you do in any worthwhile project. You say: "I've come this far, why not go all the way to the top?" Then you say: "How *do* I get myself in gear so that I can get as far up toward the top as I can?"

You discard the old, dry, fallacious statements such as, "Keep your nose to the grindstone," "Keep your shoulder to the wheel," "Keep your nose clean," "A good person will be rewarded," and "You can't keep a good person down." They sound fine but they're dated and unreal.

You're realistic enough to know that you can't afford to put your blind trust in fate. Nothing is ever going to be handed to you just because you're a nice person. *It's up to you* to struggle for what you want out of life.

Your master plan has these initial elements:

1. Your assessment of your present go-ahead powers. You have courage and competence, but your assessment of your capabilities must be made in the face of how your courage and competence are continually cut down by your hidden anxieties. Anxieties of all kinds are your "cut-down" roadblocks. Make a list of the *areas where you are very good.* Make a second list of areas where you need to strengthen yourself, *areas where you are not so good.* The main point here is to diminish your anxieties about not being successful. You have more going for you than you're aware of. Anxiety is not real, it is an emotion. *Put the real sources of courage and competence to work for you.*

2. Your outline of the positions to which you want to be promoted "along the route," so that you can move up steadily to the main position at the top where you really want to be. This, in effect, is a guessing timetable. You know *something* of what is required of you for you to hold these jobs along the way to the top. This is your work sheet for the solid preparations which you must begin to make in order to qualify for these along-the-route jobs.

3. You get off your butt and get started. You put an end to wishful thinking, to the "you-can't-beat-city-hall" excuses, to the "you-gotta-play-politics-to-move-ahead-here" dropout reason.

Of all these, the *making the persistent effort* on your part is the most important. No one is going to tap you on the shoulder time after time and tell you you've just won the "big promotion." That is Fantasy Land. Reality, the place where you and I live, is knowing where you are going and working hard to get there. For you and me there is no other way.

Using the go-ahead power that is within you

You need energy to get ahead. Where do you find it? You already have it. You just have not been using it as much as you could. You have an internal power, yours for the asking, to help you over the long stretch of the years. Others have used it since recorded time; it is not unique to you.

The president of a large industrial manufacturing company gave me these "go-ahead" power suggestions.

1. *You hurt yourself* more than anyone else can—and by *not* hurting yourself any further you can release yourself from these hampering emotions.

2. *You help yourself* most when you concentrate on your ability to succeed. You already have some successes; you want more. You obtain more successes by using your emotional control to

stress the positive thinking that you *can* succeed, instead of falling into the abyss of negative thinking that you "aren't worthy of success."

3. You study the religious fundamentals—the teachings of the centuries—to refresh your faith in yourself and in mankind.

4. You study those *who have made it*. The biographies of many successful business people are easily available. Most business publications carry articles on top executives. How did these individuals accomplish it? What can you learn from them?

5. You accept the rules for *treating yourself like a human being* so that you can bring out the best that is in you. When you're your own worst enemy, blocking yourself with unnecessary depression and guilt feelings, you're not treating yourself like a human being. You're sadistically depriving yourself of the energy you need to move upward by using it to beat your internal self into a quivering mess.

6. You *sharpen your insight* by doing a lot of thinking on the subject. *Why* are you as you are? *What* makes you tick? *Where* did you get the emotional hang-ups you have? Even though you realize everyone else has emotional problems why do *you* have the ones that plague you? Knowing they are there, understanding them, enables you to cope with them—to diminish their effect on you.

7. You sharpen your insight into *other people* for the same reason; greater understanding of human behavior is one of your strongest assets as an executive.

8. You tighten your grip on this thought: *"I'm going to make it* because I want to control my own destiny. I want to know who I am, to understand myself, to find my real identity in success."

Power within you? There is a great deal of it. The president I referred to used all this power. You can surprise yourself by unlocking the doors that have kept it from use. Emotional doors based on unreality.

No one can keep you back except yourself.

Knowing this, you use the powers of ambition, love of

achievement, true appreciation of yourself, to win what you deserve—a place at the top.

Selecting your opportunities for gaining attention

Hiding your light under a bushel basket went out of style around the turn of the century. It won't do you a bit of good today, either.

An insurance executive put it this way: "You must make yourself more visible to your boss and to the top executives above you." *Your* opportunities for preparing yourself for more attention are clearly wrapped up in these basic elements of American business:

- Making more profits—the name of the game
- Manufacturing products at less cost
- Distributing, marketing, and selling products with greater efficiency
- Sharper management of money
- More productive management of people
- More intelligent use of data and information on which to base decisions

Concentrate on one after another of these subjects over a period of time. Learn as much as you can about them. Find ways and means to generate your own ideas of how the company can do better in *any* of them.

Innovative, imaginative ideas on how to do something to increase profits will always gain attention for you—and respect.

An insurance executive makes more than $60,000 a year, base salary. *He* didn't hide his light. Why should *you?*

Helping the spotlight to find you

In addition to your ideas of how things can be done better, which indicate your grasp of the business, *your record is on show.* Top management for the most part is busy in many other areas. They rely on a periodic look at your record to see how well *you* are doing in non-office activities as well as in your assigned duties.

"People's out-of-the-office records are a fine way of revealing that they are indispensable managers who show great promise of developing into excellent executives," the head of a steel fabricating firm told me. "They are showing the people at the top that they have also grasped the idea of how *business professionals* conduct themselves." Excellent point.

Not only are you judged by the clothes you wear and how well you wear them but by the way you conduct yourself and the way you express yourself. Your membership and contributions to your church, business organizations, industry groups, civic and fraternal clubs, sports activities, the arts and social groups, all are taken into consideration.

Since they are going to judge you by your record of what you do *in* the office and what you do *outside* the office, give them a splendid record to look at!

Being involved in these activities takes time (perhaps too much time), but it is part of your plan to draw the spotlight of top management to you and to develop your skills of working with other people. Being "involved" in respectable non-office activities helps train you in human relations and solving people-oriented problems.

Perfecting the art of being organized

To be organized is to be efficient. The executive vice president of a national business association said: "Efficiency means that you know your job very well, that you've got the workload laid out efficiently, and that the work is being done."

"It means," she added, "that you are a 'take-charge' person who can keep a sharp eye on the projects under way, who wins the respect of employees by setting a good example and using tact and diplomacy with everyone."

You can be as efficient as anyone. It takes effort, but you're well aware of that. You work hard at setting up the goals of your department, of breaking them down into attainable objectives. You work at short- and long-range planning to achieve these objectives. You arm yourself with the strongest type of forecasting methods that you can devise so that you'll have a clearer idea of where you're going.

As for your group of subordinates, you're organized very well with them. You discuss their work performance as individuals and as a group, and you establish sensible criteria for deciding what they should measure up to. You keep them in an "achievement-minded" state of action; because of your efficiency you enable them to score more achievements —individually (which they like) and in a group (which your superiors like).

Strengthening your organization – for your benefit

Another way that you are judged by those at the top is by the quality of the people you hire in your group and how well you train them. "This is a point a lot of managers fail to take note of," a retired chief officer of a chemical company emphasized during an interview. "You can't just hire people and let them vegetate. You must employ the brightest people you can find, those who will bring in freshness of ideas and a desire to find new ways to do the work."

If you hire people who are much like you in personality, you'll end up with a mess on your hands. You *need* subordinates who aren't afraid to push and jostle you, who want to try new methods and techniques, who can help you think and plan ahead. It is your task to coach these men and women so that they become a unified working group, with each person involved and committed to participating enthusiastically.

Sound like a dream? No one said it was *easy,* only that it was your responsibility to work with them to bring out their best. You establish two-way communication—and you listen to them. You build up their self-esteem. You emphasize rewarding them instead of running a "tight ship" where punishment is always in store for anyone who gets the slightest bit out of line with you.

You give them freedom in an atmosphere where they know they can talk to you without fear of being put down. You are flexible in your dealings with them. You accept and study their ideas and suggestions. You put things on their level of intelligence so that you're not talking over their heads.

Whatever you do to strengthen the people who work with you, you strengthen yourself. More managers should understand this fact. That's what the retired chief officer was getting at.

You understand it, and you'll make it work for you.

Building your ability to handle trouble

Who needs trouble? No one. We'd all like to get along without it. But problems come whether we want them or not. This point was underscored by a senior vice president ($85,000 bracket) of a materials-handling equipment company during a lunch we had together.

Handling problems (trouble) is your job. You've handled many problems before today. How do you build your ability to handle more in the future? The senior vice president offered these pointers for you to keep in mind:

1. Since you realize you cannot escape problems you settle yourself down to be a professional problem solver, a troubleshooter who is smart enough to smell out potential problem areas. Being prepared is half the battle.

2. If problems aren't solved quickly and lastingly they become holes down which corporate profits can drop. Losing money isn't happily accepted. Clearing up problems *can* help profits. You don't really have a choice.

3. You make a careful, honest appraisal of your people. Where might there be profit leaks because of poor work habits or breakdown in intergroup communications? How many have more work stacked on their desk than they can handle? Who is lethargic and a bottleneck for the work flow? What changes can you make to prevent troubles from cropping up in your group?

4. Share your burden with your people. Tell them that *they* have a piece of the action in preventing troubles and in clearing up problems before they become grotesque messes. Tell them to bring in their ideas and suggestions any time of the day. The more they help the more you're equipped to handle troubles

5. Don't allow a flow of problem solving to whip by you without studying what is going on. Where are the troubles coming from? How often? What can you do to stem or lessen the flow? Is one person the cause, or more than one? Is it a work mechanic that is the source of the troubles, a technique that isn't working, a system that's fallen apart? What? Study the action and get to the root cause.

Doing what you can to step up productivity

Make people work harder? You're kidding!

I'm not kidding, nor are the people at the top. They want you to put some muscle into an on-the-job training program to get more productivity out of your people. At the same time, they want you to develop in your people a greater faith in the corporation.

Work harder and be more enthusiastic about the company? It can be done. You can work with your people to increase their work output and still develop their greater trust and confidence in the company.

Here's how a vice president of an automotive supply company suggested that you do it:

1. Demonstrate to your people that *you are interested in them*. They'll work a bit harder when they realize they aren't being

ignored, that you have a sympathetic understanding of their duties and the problems involved in getting their work done. Paying attention to people in a moderate, not-too-pushy way is still essential to your good relations with them. You'll see their work output rise if you find appropriate ways to show them that you are interested in them *as individuals,* not as work units.

2. Work out specific areas in which some of your people are to be *trained on the job.* Not everyone will come to your group fully qualified. You're the coach, so start coaching. You won't like spending the time on it, but you'll like the results—more productivity.

3. Make certain your communication lines to them are open, that you have *two-way communications.* Talk to them individually or in small units and discuss the group's overall problems and *the role each person plays* in the group's success. Assure them that they can come to you at any time with ideas, suggestions, comments, criticisms.

4. Set up *emergency procedures* so that everyone working for you understands that serious troubles can develop without warning and so that *everyone shares your concern in settling them quickly.* I know of some managers who have held "fire drills" on this subject during which they present make-believe troubles to their assembled subordinates. They work out the "solving procedures" right then and there. The main thing is to shake up your people, startle them a bit, get them to be trouble-solving-oriented, so that when a biggie comes your way you're not all stunned into inaction. "Fire drills" can teach everyone in your group how to put out fires. Do that and your group productivity won't suffer because of slipshod handling of emergencies.

5. *Bring in all the help you can get.* Many associations, such as the National Association of Manufacturers, the Council of Profit Sharing Industries, and the state manufacturing associations, have filmstrips, booklets, literature, 35-mm slide presentations, and the like available to help you put specific messages across to your people. Use them whenever you feel they are appropriate.

A little showmanship won't hurt a bit. The men and women in your group will feel you've made extra effort to pay attention to them, and they'll respond.

6. *Get feedback.* You're trying to step up productivity. You've been ordered not to hire any more people but to handle a larger workload in your group, as a step to help increase corporate profits. Nothing wrong with this, but *how is it going over with your subordinates?* Do they understand why? Are they hiding resentment? Find out. Talk to them, and do it frequently. Get the type of feedback from them which will help you analyze whether *you* are handling things effectively or if there is more you should be doing to persuade them to increase their output.

7. "Team spirit" is a term you've heard often; it refers to an elusive quality. Most people don't regard themselves a "part of a team," even though they may mouth the words. They are individuals. To get them to function with a team spirit" *you must play to their individuality.* You must give each person his or her due time and attention. You must present your ideas and messages, your instructions, to them in a way that is related to their individual needs. Few people are sparked by the same motivations. You learn what makes each person respond well, what level you can reach him or her on, and you use this 'what-they-need" avenue to move people toward your goals. Any other way means failure.

Yes, *you can persuade people to use their full working abilities* at the office or the plant. When top management talks about *stepping up productivity* they don't mean using a whip or forcing people to drop in exhaustion. They mean getting people to do a *normal, fair share of work each day.* The reverse side of the coin is the fact that many people *do not* put out a normal, fair day's work. They slow down, procrastinate, tend to personal affairs, waste time, create more work by being thoughtless and by making mistakes.

You step up work output a bit when you teach your people that they can work to the best of their abilities and *be appreciated.* You show them that there are rewards of recognition for those who perform satisfactorily, that those who don't will have to shape up or ship out.

You can't leave it up to your subordinates. *You're the manager.* Go ahead and manage them into doing more and better work!

The vice president who helped me with these "productivity pointers" has moved from $20,000 to $42,000 in less than ten years. It's possible for *you* to do the same.

Use this yardstick for measuring your own maturity

We all think we're mature. After all, we're not kids any more. Okay, how mature *are* you? How many of the following statements is true of you?

1. I'm never abrasive to anyone.

2. I refuse to be one of those overbearing people who act as if they know everything and talk only to God.

3. I value my personal integrity.

4. I value the historic virtues of our American way of life and despite some of our national problems I feel honored to be a citizen of this country.

5. I like the idea of being imaginative, of finding new ways to do old methods better, of trying out new ideas and techniques.

6. I am sensitive to other people, knowing that I must be tolerant of them as individuals, that none of them are cast in my image, that each has weaknesses and strengths, that I must accept them the way they are and help them to increase their strengths.

7. I can stick it out, knowing that there will be times I'll wish I'd stayed in bed, but that I'm being paid to handle the rough times as well as the good times. If things go wrong I'll try to find

out why and be better prepared the next time. Resiliency, the ability to bounce back and go on to the next order of things, is part of my bag.

8. I have self-control, which includes patience to let things work out the way I want them to. I won't lose my cool over unimportant matters. I'll be highly organized, so that I can cut down the amount of "unauthorized troubles" that arrive at my desk which would make me pop my cork.

9. I identify with my corporation. I don't bite the hand that feeds me. *Here* is where I can make it. I'll develop my people and I'll develop myself. My corporation will benefit and we will all benefit.

10. I am an individual out to do everything I can for myself and my family. There is nothing wrong with this attitude. It gives me confidence and impetus to try to move up into the executive suite, to gain the recognition I feel I deserve, to share some of the goodies at the top.

11. I am a politician in the sense that I know I can't achieve miracles by will power alone. I realize that people have a habit of getting in the way, that "people troubles" come when least expected. I know that I can't change things overnight. In all practicality it takes months and years to effect substantial changes in people, practices, and systems. I bide my time politically, doing as much as I can, gaining everyone's confidence and trust in me, and building my strength of character and my management abilities.

12. Finally, I have perseverance. Call it "staying power" or whatever. The fact is I've made up my mind to get as high in this corporate world as I can. I know I must earn the right to each promotion, but I'll persevere in my efforts no matter how many roadblocks I meet (even those I may create emotionally within me).

If most of these statements apply to you, you have the right idea. You have the maturity which will take you on to those salaries in the executive suite. The individuals who today are making $40,000 to $70,000 at the top are persons who possess most of these same mature features.

Checking out the people who are ahead of you

Who are these people who are taking home all that loot? How did they get where they are? What did they do to win those big offices and big salaries?

You want to get to the top and you have every right to work in that direction. Some of these people may be in your way. Some of them may accept you and help make room for you. Others might not take too kindly to you. Some of them might not be around by the time you arrive in the executive suite. It will pay you to take some time and make a written appraisal of these top individuals in your corporation and the qualities (good and bad) which you see in them.

Do it this way:

1. Write down their abilities as you perceive them.
2. Write down their character deficiencies as you see them.
3. Write down the "successes" for which they have been noted. Those you know. What have they done that was outstanding, unique, really great?
4. What helped them get where they are? Nepotism? Special training? Special capabilities? Powerful friends?
5. Which ones are the innovators, the ones who seem to come up with fresh ways of looking at things and getting things done?
6. Which ones are the most persuasive? How do they sell their ideas and concepts to the rest of the executive group?
7. Which ones seem to be deadwood and might be pushed out before long? Why are they in trouble?
8. What would you guess is the motivational complex behind each of these people? What drives do they have that you can discover?
9. Which ones are the potential *helpers* for you and the potential *roadblocks for you?* Why would they be either one?

10. How do these executives regard the corporation? With extreme loyalty? Do they conceal their feelings by not saying much of anything?

All this will give you an idea of who is on first, second, and third in the game of getting yourself into the executive suite. You'll be a bit hampered by lack of all the facts at the outset, but with persistence you can build a file over a period of time. You are wise to know *who* is in the job you want, *how* this person got there, *what* he or she is doing to keep the job, and what you can benefit from by studying this individual's conduct.

This isn't lightweight espionage. You have every right to know as much about the people at the top as you can reasonably find out. These are the ones making the big decisions. Your study of them as "those who made it" and "those who are running things" is essential to your understanding of what will be expected of *you* when you reach equal status with some of them.

Knowing where you're going and who's there ahead of you is important to your successful approach toward the top.

Making a working list of rules for your daily conduct

While you're studying other people they are studying *you*. You are always on show. It will help you immeasurably to have some good workable rules in your mental hip pocket to get you through each day so that your bright side shows through and the bad side is held in check. (Why blow things with a display of temper?)

Think about these simple but highly effective rules of conduct:

1. I will pace myself and not take on more work than I can handle. If I overload myself, I'll become tense and irritable and won't be able to work at my best.

2. I'll make my decisions as expertly as I can and not worry myself to death about them. I'll go on to the next order of business.

3. I'll keep a finger on the pulse of my subordinates by listening to them, both as to what they say and *what they don't say*.

4. With all my emphasis on good professional management, I still won't kid myself that I can accomplish miracles simply by being a good manager. Each day is different. I must know my people and the limitations against getting all kinds of work done through them. I may have to bring in extra help, or specialized help, from time to time.

5. No matter how much I like to have help, I am the one who has the job of making myself known as a mover, a person who gets things done. I won't look to others to establish this reputation for me.

6. I'll be conscious of time, a very precious commodity when I'm trying to get a lot of things done. Making the best use of my time is essential to my growth as a manager.

7. I'll tell the truth consistent with not tipping top management's hand on a particular subject. If I don't weave webs to deceive I won't get caught in the tangled threads.

8. I'll fight natural anxiety by reminding myself that my job is secure as long as I perform satisfactorily and am not insubordinate to my boss.

9. I'll perform satisfactorily by working hard each day, not just once in a while. I'll work hard at what I'm being paid to do, solve problems, manage people, manage myself, get the work done.

10. I'll stay out of the shadows by keeping myself on top of what's going on in my company, in the industry we serve, and in the nation generally. Becoming aware of what's going on, both through reading widely and through discussions with alert people, is very important to me.

11. I'll treat everyone with sympathetic understanding, giving credit where it is due, making allowances where they are justified.

12. I know there will be times when the going will be tough. I'll keep myself under control. I won't lose my temper, become irritated, or feel that any problem is personally aimed at me.

13. I'll learn from the older managers. They've been doing some things right, and I want to know what those things are.

14. I figure most people will like me and I'll like them. It's up to

me to make the first friendly move. I'll think better of other people if I concentrate on their good features, not their bad ones.

15. I'll have faith in myself. I've come this far, I can go further. I'm in a race with time, but I can't rush things. I must develop more and more self-control and learn more about managing other people and equipping myself to become a good executive. I'm no longer searching for an identity—I have it. Now I'm searching for significant achievements and a place at the top.

16. I'm aware that I'm actually spending my lifetime developing myself into a specific character. I am *me,* unmistakably a real individual.

17. I'll bring into my group as many people as I can rely upon to work satisfactorily. I want people who can grow through my coaching and training and who will consider me an exacting boss but a fair one.

18. I'll use differenct types and combinations of incentives to perk up my people. These will include reasonable pay raises, praise when it is due, and acceptance of them as individuals with their own talents and skills. I'll use other human relations techniques to show them that I appreciate them and what they're doing in the group.

That's a long list of rules of conduct, but you could add many more of your own to it.

The results of putting this knowledge to work for you are visible when

- You *know* you have established good working relationships with the other wheels in the organization.
- You *know* that you are held in high esteem by most of the people with whom you work.
- You *know* that you are capable of influencing some of the top people by your articulateness and possession of facts.
- Some of the other top dogs come to you *for your advice* on how to handle things.
- You are in a meeting and *contribute your share* of ideas and suggestions.

- You have made decisions you know were the *right* ones.
- You *know* you have succeeded in motivating one or more of your subordinates effectively.
- You know that you've overcome the human relations problem and that your subordinates *are working closely with you.*
- You *know* you've made the most of your time each day.
- You find you've been working well *under pressure.*
- You wake up and find you're really *happy* to be going to work.
- You know that by *controlling your emotions* you are controlling your rise upward in the organization.

Your rules are tailored to suit you and to help you get where you want to go. Rules such as these are merely part of knowing where you want to go. The way to the top is paved, not with good intentions, but with good daily working rules.

Checking yourself out for "emotional common sense"

No one will ever agree what common sense is. But the wisdom of "emotional common sense" is universally recognized because controlling one's emotions *is* a universal challenge.

Dozens of the executives I talked to all agreed that in the business world *you* must create within yourself a "growing" understanding of what it means to develop common sense in the management field. There are these stages of growth:

1. You first become aware of how much there is to know about business. *You don't feel personally involved,* but you're intrigued with the immenseness of the challenges. You begin to see that you have been doing some things wrong and a few things right.

2. Then, sometime later, when you arrive at the point where you are deeply concerned with yourself *and* with other people, *you find you have become involved.* You suddenly become more aware of your deficiencies in the business world, in the way you

treat yourself and in the way you treat others. You are bothered. You start to pry further into the business world to see how you can do things better. You are eager to change yourself to meet the challenges.

3. Lastly, you reach a stage where *you have learned* how to control some or most of your emotions, to understand more about yourself and others. You begin to see how you can put this enormously valuable knowledge to work for you in moving up the staircase of success.

Your emotional common sense is nothing more than maturity. Some people, as you know, never achieve it. Others seem to have had it from childhood. *As it applies to you,* now is the time when you put it to work the hardest. Now is the time when you use everything you have learned about human nature to help push you upward to the top.

Grappling with the large-corporation problems

It takes a little something special in the way of emotional common sense to work in a big corporation. The very size of the monster makes it nearly impossible for you to find out what someone else or some other department is doing. It makes it difficult to communicate with your boss and with others and for them to communicate effectively with you.

Because there are so many people, there naturally is more competition for the available promotions. Talk about conflict! The size of the corporation tends to pull people apart rather than draw them together. You get the feeling that everyone is out for herself and himself. Personality problems develop over the simplest things, sometimes over childish ones.

If you are in a large corporation you'll have to fight these divisive factors. You'll have to fight the overpowering feeling of frustration about making yourself heard, about the difficulty of drawing the spotlight of attention to you, about winning solid recognition for your work well done.

As a manager you have more pressure on you to produce. Despite any reasonable excuses you may have, the corporation wields a pretty big whip (of indifference to excuses) to make you produce more and help create more profits. The unspoken admonition is unmistakably, "If you can't do it, we'll get someone who will."

"You look around at the hungry ones who'd like to have your job, and you feel mighty lonely and isolated," one corporation vice president confessed. "That system of produce-or-else, plus the fact that large corporations are enormously complicated, with highly involved technologies, makes anyone's game plan of getting to the top excruciatingly more difficult. Politics, which exists everywhere, exists in its hottest sense in large corporations."

Below the surface there are jealousies, intrigues, rivalries, undermining, conspiracies, intense personal competition, "placing-the-blame" setups, and all the other ugly human nature components. It is an atmosphere in which you must exist and still succeed.

Despite all this the use of the proper "positive" emotions will help you in your task. You know what these are, but let me list the main ones anyway:

1. Desire to be creative and innovative
2. A feeling of being vigorous, alive, vital
3. Conviction that you're going to make it
4. Enthusiasm for doing any job, large or small
5. A sense of urgency that time isn't waiting for you, it's hurrying you along
6. Optimism that you, your group, and your corporation are all going to do very well together
7. Eagerness to accomplish many difficult things
8. Courage to state your views when you feel them appropriate
9. Patience because you know that you can't move everything at once
10. Adaptability to meet the changing scenes and demands
11. Persistence in moving yourself upwards
12. Inspiration which you give to others

13. Judgment (gained as a result of all your experiences) which you put to work for you each day

14. Self-discipline to get your work done, on time, the way it should be done

15. Self-control so that you can objectively manage the work of other people and remain pleasant, courteous, and helpful to them all.

The editing of your master plan for getting yourself going

The world isn't going to wait around for you. You can't get to the top on hope alone; you must work for it. A general manager of a branch plant stressed it this way: "Set your sights on what you honestly feel you can achieve. If it's the presidency, *go for it*. If it's a vice presidency, *go for that*."

You must bring into each of your days as many stimuli as you can muster to keep prodding you in your master plan. Talk to people whom you respect, associate with the kind of people you admire, who have made it, who can help establish within you the "I-can-make-it" attitude.

Stay away from whatever gets under your skin and irritates or depresses you. Spend your time working in the positive areas and keep the negative, unappealing areas to a minimum.

Stop coasting. You're in a race with time. Grab for and use every sensible method or technique you come across. Read about, or see with your own eyes, how other people do it. Try as many innovations as you can get away with.

Fight the tendency to play it safe. Your career can come to rest in some backwater office if you don't exert yourself. You'll sit there, unhappy, deep in depression, aware that the game has gone by you *because you allowed yourself to be blocked and uncompetitive*.

If you feel you're "tied down" where you are, *get yourself untied*. The bureaucratic systems of corporations can work to tie down almost everyone, but *you* don't have to hold still for it. Make your moves. Show the people at the top that you've got resources they can use to benefit the corporation.

When you're working on a project, don't wander away from it. Fasten your mind to what you're supposed to be doing. Cut off phone conversations and other meaningless talk, and stay with the problem until you have one or more solutions. Then put the most obvious solution into the works.

The world of business isn't constructed for you to get "instant approval" or 'instant promotion" for every good thing you do. You know this. Rely on your overall track record to do the most effective speaking for you. Recognition comes in many forms, and you'll know when you get it (usually without fanfare).When you stop thinking like an employee and *think like a manager* you're on your way to becoming a manager. When you stop thinking purely like a manager and start seeing things the way an executive does, you're on your way to becoming an executive.

Whatever else you do, finding ways to *motivate* your people to do creditable, substantial work is your most important achievement.

You sensibly reject the feeling of "not belonging" or of "not being in the in group." You know that this is simply a feeling, not a fact. You can earn your way into acceptance by individuals and by the in group simply by working consistently and having a master plan that is wisely constructed.

Your master plan is somewhat like the map to a gold mine. Without a firm plan of knowing where you're going, you'll most likely drift around in the business world. With it, you have the resolution and the impetus to make it upward from one manager's job to another until you have worked your way up to where you want to be—in gold-mine country.

The executive suite is extremely difficult to get into. That's why you can't trust fate or luck to get you there. Trust yourself.

Now get started on laying out your master plan. Do that *now;* then let's see what else you can do to speed up your progress to the top, your rise from a low or medium income bracket into one somewhere between the $25,000 and $50,000 spread.

After all, one of the measures of how well your master plan can work is how high up in the income area you can move. Why let someone else get the title and the money?

CHAPTER FIVE

Removing the No. 1 Stumbling Block— Human Conflict

You've decided you can make it pretty high up the ladder. And you *can*.

You've put together your own master plan for reaching the top. It *will* work.

Only *you* can keep yourself from the top job you want. If you give up, or falter, or sink into self-pity, or really fumble, then you beat yourself. There is no need for this. You *can* control yourself, as we have seen in the previous chapters. You *can* arm yourself with the tools and expertise you need.

The unpredictable roadblocks which can cause you problems on your way up are mostly centered in human conflict.

Why are human beings so much in conflict in the office and the plant?

Understanding the WHY of human conflict

There is an endless list of factors that separate one human being from another. You've already become familiar with some of them. You've felt these divisive emotions yourself, often with an accompanying wonder of *why* you felt that way.

You know that two reasonable people should never be in conflict with each other. There is no need for conflicts; they can usually settle the problem between them in an intellectual, unhostile way.

But most human beings are not reasonable all the time. Your experience with others has included many unhappy instances in which people were highly unreasonable in their demands on you.

You thought the demands were unreasonable. The other people argued that they *were* reasonable. So—more human conflict.

It is this type of conflict which can cause you serious trouble in reaching the top unless you learn how to avoid it or how to diminish its impact on your career. In the business world there seldom is a "kiss-and-make-up" aftermath of a good, hot, brawling conflict.

You can accept this. Human beings, it is said, carry within them ancient seeds of conflict with one another, seeds that started back at the dawning of time. The fact that we've evolved into the twenty-first century doesn't dilute the massive evidence of mankind's apparent inability to avoid conflict—the wars, the uprisings, the takeovers of power, the assassinations, the brutal periods such as the witch hunts, the Inquisition, the treatment of the American Indians, the German concentration camps, the Russian slave-labor camps.

Nevertheless, conflict between two individuals is avoidable if both of them possess *awareness* of the dangers of their hidden hostilities. Conflict is not avoidable if an individual is still uncontrollably governed by an unconscious desire to vent hostilities on someone else.

How do you understand the components of human conflict so that you can avoid slipping into trouble with other people and thereby harming yourself? How can you use this awareness to help you in your efforts to become a top-flight executive?

Let's examine some of the intense emotional problems that plague most of us and make human cooperation sometimes difficult.

Why most people haven't used their full potentials

You've heard the expression, "We're our own worst enemies." How true!

"In the years that I've been in the business world I've met many people who seem to be going nowhere," a corporation president said during an interview. 'These are people who have exerted themselves just enough to stay afloat in a job and no more. I've met very few men and women proportionately who have used *all* their positive potentials to get ahead. Many of them seem to be doing things which *keep* them from being more successful."

Why?

First, almost all of us harbor in our unconscious mind some deep feelings that we're really not worth very much. Things happened to us in our early lives which conditioned us to feel that we were *not* entitled to win any successes or gain anything of value. We feel guilt no matter how trivial our successes or how small the thing of value that we obtain. How these *feelings of unworthiness and guilt* get into us is a subject for someone far more qualified than I am. *They are in us,* and you and I know they are.

Second, because we feel unworthy and guilty when something good happens to us, we are caught up in a recurring cycle of self-defeatism. It never seems to let us go. The more successful some people become, the deeper their feeling of self-defeat.

Anthony Quinn, on a Johnny Carson TV show, said that at the time when he had three movies showing on Broadway and was starring with Sir Laurence Olivier in *Becket*, he "felt he needed help" from a psychiatrist. His self-defeat mechanism was working too strongly for him to handle what anyone else would regard as "top success."

There is something about the growing-up process when we're children that gives many of us *a feeling that we're not significant*. We're small, not aware of life fully, without any resources of our own, under the control of our parents and teachers, and, in a sense, helpless. We carry this feeling into adulthood in our unconscious. We can't seem to forget the humiliations of those helpless times. It is ingrained in our characters that we don't deserve anything special. In the business world this tendency to respond to the hidden poisons of self-defeat is not overly obvious in most people. But you as an executive-in-training must learn to recognize it in yourself and in others—and to cope with it.

It is a shock to all of us to come to understand that not everyone is working at full speed to become a success. This fact alone might be enough to assure *your* success because so many others default from the race.

Emotions that cause people to "hang fire" in their business lives

There are emotions other than self-defeat which cause many people to hang fire all their business lives. They have good educational backgrounds and are experienced in business but never seem to step off and get going.

The following emotions are as insidious and hidden as self-defeat, and they do as much damage:

1. *Resentment of any authority figure.* Stemming from their dislike of a parent, an older brother or sister, or a relative, this emotion is transferred unwittingly to all bosses. It makes it tough

for the bosses but much more difficult for the holder of the resentment.

2. *Guilt*. Everyone sets out with a dream of what he or she wants to be in life. Those who don't realize their "dream existence," and there are hordes of them, cut themselves to ribbons emotionally because they didn't become what they had most deeply wanted to be. In their emotional center they are failures. They berate themselves for not having made use of their potentials to become creative persons. To their way of looking at it they have wasted their lives and done little to achieve what they really wanted. Their sense of guilt is enormous.

3. *Anxiety*. Previously we discussed the uselessness of this emotion. Anxiety is not based on a real fact in any way, shape, or form. Yet nearly all of us suffer from it. It makes us feel lonely, helpless, without power, fearful that something terrible is going to happen to us at any minute. It often keeps us from trying something really worthwhile because we fear failure. Many of us repeatedly back away from certain activities which could lead to conditions where we *know* we'd become extremely anxious. For example: Giving a speech, being in a play, appearing on a TV interview program, speaking out at a town hall meeting. Many of us protect ourselves so well from anxiety that we hurt ourselves more than we could possibly be hurt by the "danger" which led to our anxiety in the first place.

4. *Perfectionism*. This is anxiety in another of its disguises. Perfectionists don't have much confidence. In fact they feel fairly worthless. They are motivated to rise as high as they can so that they'll escape criticism and find some small sense of security from being near the top. They bolster their shaky egos by looking down on others, finding fault with everyone and everything, building dossiers on certain people so they can show that others are less than perfect. They pretend they are seeking the perfect solution when in fact they are avoiding making any decision at all. They would rather have others deal with the problem so that they

could then find fault with the way they did it. People who work for perfectionists find it difficult to realize that they are just frightened creatures with big loads of anxiety.

5. *Depression.* Who hasn't felt this from time to time? There are many people who are never free from it. It is their dominating emotion, one which devours them. They have no faith in themselves. They feel very lonely and unworthy and are tormented by the conviction that they can't win at anything. When they make a minor mistake, often unnoticed, they take it to heart with great pain. They worry about it for an unnecessarily long period of time. They berate themselves for their failure—which by this time they've blown up to a size all out of proportion to the original trivial mistake. They spend so much of their energy feeling depressed that they succumb to fatigue, lassitude, apathy, and discouragement.

6. *Neuroticism.* This is another face of anxiety, showing itself through depression but more dramatically. Neurotics in business just can't handle the tough ones. They start to feel aggressive, ready to tackle a big assignment, and their neuroticism clicks in and overwhelms them. They'll have a fit of anger. They'll say irritable things. In the end they'll do anything except sustain their aggressive work.

This short list is enough. It shows you as a manager and as an executive-in-training that people are a great deal more complicated than most of us realize. How can you tell who is neurotic, who is depressed, who is the perfectionist, who is the anxious, guilty, authority-hating person?

Look around you. Nearly everyone has one of these tendencies.

There are some tell-tale clues, some tip-offs, to each of the emotional conditions. People don't usually wear their emotions out in the open where you can see them. They're inside, working like mad to keep their victims from being happy and successful.

You must know how to handle subordinates who are governed by these and other emotions.

How you can understand your subordinates' hidden emotions

Get ready for a lifetime of trying.

Much has been published about the emotional effects on people who are crowded into big cities and who work in organizations with many other people. We know that overcrowding makes people hostile to one another. The human being is a territory-minded creature and if the space immediately around is invaded the human feels hostile and will even *act* hostile!

People in business organizations often have this hemmed-in feeling. Coupled with the feeling that they aren't accepted by the group and amount to nothing in the organization, it can make some of them enormously hostile inside, to the point where they have difficulty concealing it.

Every man or woman in business feels a touch lonely, a touch defenseless, perhaps vulnerable. We all feel that we need some weapon with which to protect ourselves. Among the attitudes and techniques that people unconsciously develop in response to this feeling are the following:

1. *Agression.* It is one of our most valuable ancestral emotions. It prompts us to move out and do things for our own benefit. It was our agression that made us break away from the domination of our parents. It made us pry into strange corners when we were young. It took us into education and made us try for top grades and honors. It took us into athletic competitions where we could prove our superiority. Because of aggression, we are all competitors of one another. Because of our aggression, we have established our own identity among other people and with ourselves. Without an aggressive springboard, we would venture very little, attempt nothing risky.

2. *Autonomy.* This is one of the more visible weapons because we do things that make it obvious. All of us live in fear that we'll be rejected by an individual or by a group. We all fear looking ridiculous because of failing at something when someone is

watching. We value our identity, but strangely we won't share it with anyone. If a man or woman approaches us intimately we tend to back away, to be frightened emotionally. We *know* we need other people around because who wants to be lonely? But when they come too close to our emotional center, our alarms go off and we feel somehow threatened. If we allow a person to get too close to us, we'll lose our autonomy. So we react and do all we can to retain our individuality. Like nations, we need someone to project ourselves against; I'm the good character and he's the bad character. We'll find someone we can hang the bad-character label on, even if it is far-fetched. We have to have an enemy to prove that we're important.

3. *Ego.* A psychiatrist can tell you more about this than I can. I do know that it is a powerful force within people, making them move into areas of endeavor where the more faint-hearted fear to tread. But a price is paid. With every ego there is the problem of its unquenchable appetite for more recognition, more pats on the back, more huzzahs, more favorable treatment.

4. *Self-esteem.* Yes, despite the negative emotions, people still are capable of feeling self-esteem. Some go through a valley of being hampered by negative emotions, then find a way to the top of an emotional hill where they find they like themselves. And because they aren't busy wasting emotions feeling sorry for themselves, or depressed, or angry, or fearful, they can spend that energy doing creative things. These are the lucky ones!

5. *Domination.* Even a subordinate can dominate you if he or she is so motivated. Many men and women are motivated to be in a dominating position no matter how small or insignificant it might be. This type of domination can be of two types. One is the forceful "I'm-bigger-and-more-important-than-you-are"kind to which some top managers and executives resort. The other is the attempt a person makes to dominate you indirectly by allowing himself, or herself, to be defeated. *How's that?* For example, a secretary is supposed to do typing and filing. He either doesn't do them, or does them poorly. He gains a reverse sort of power over

you by *not* performing to your standards. You are forced to spend an extra amount of time with him, or because of him. You've been dominated, whether you know it or not.

6. *Self-hate.* This is a useless emotion, but it exists within many men and women. They hate themselves because in childhood they were somehow taught that they were no good, worthless, not wanted, that somebody else was better and more nearly perfect. These unfortunate people manage to live and grow, but there is a painful price to pay for the acid eating inside them. They hate themselves, have no confidence in themselves. What do they do when they feel this terrible pain? Some become heavy drinkers. Some run through dozens of affairs. Others figuratively lie down and let the world walk all over them. Whatever the punishment is, they feel they deserve it.

7. *Comparison.* Some people keep themselves in a self-defeating state by always comparing themselves to other workers, managers, executives, and relatives and friends. This is one of the most caustic mental activities anyone can engage in. If you continually compare yourself with others, you'll never win because *they* will always appear to have more than you do, to be more successful, to have escaped the hard work and problems you've had. Don't believe it. You're basing your comparisons on inadequate information. You don't *know* whether they *are* better off than you are. If you knew the truth, they probably aren't. Your mistake is in making *any* comparisons at all. Let other people have what they have. Go after the things that are meaningful for *you*. Why hurt yourself by making comparisons that result in your feeling anxious, inadequate, unworthy, and not as successful as someone else? How ridiculous can you get?

8. *Projection.* We're all guilty of this, particularly with movie stars, politicians, and other public figures. We give them credit for all sorts of powers and qualities which they don't possess and don't deserve. In the office, some employees will project into a boss or a coworker some of their own emotions and characteristics. They will say, "I don't get upset easily, but *she* sure does!"

Or, "I'm not an office politician, but *that* guy is a real slick promoter who's just out for himself." And they'll do this without a shred of evidence.

9. *Regression.* It means just what it sounds like. People sometimes regress into their favorite childhood ways of looking at things, many of them pouty and some of them downright mean. They'll say "He's getting all the good things, and I *hate* him!" Or, "She doesn't pay as much attention to me as she does to Harry. She's trying to make my life difficult. I don't like her!" All this is in their imagination, but it may as well be real. They regress and are uncooperative, often sullen and disagreeable.

10. *Guilt.* Most people don't feel guilt consciously, but in the *unconscious,* watch out. There is no need for guilt because there are few normal human conditions which require a person actually *to feel* legitimate guilt. It is groundless. Your unconscious says, "Feel guilty!" and you respond even though there are no facts to back up the unconscious demand. The psychologists say, "The unconscious judges the self." What you're doing, if you get caught in the guilt trap, is judging yourself, finding yourself guilty, and sentencing yourself to a guilty feeling—all without any relation to reality. You pay the price—you feel bad, worthless, a sinner, a fugitive from justice, whatever. Isn't guilt stupid?

11. *Procrastination.* A long word for "putting off what could be done right now." Why do people do this? Because in an unconscious way they are trying to control you by not making decisions and being slow in doing their work. "I'll get back at you by not doing what you want me to do," they are saying with their actions. They give the appearance of being lazy and unresponsive; they are actually trying to gain control of you.

This is just a starter list of some of the most basic defense devices that you will encounter as a manager of people, as an in-training executive. The many versions of these devices will put you to the real test of understanding people As long as you're in business you'll be dealing with people and their emotional hang-ups and reactions. No way out. The more you understand what's behind their actions, the more capable you become in managing people.

How to deal with subordinates and their emotions

"Those are my sentiments" is a way people have of saying what their emotions are. "I hate that!" "I don't like it very much." "I'm not impressed." "I'm turned off by that." "Isn't that stupid?" "Who does he think he is?" There are many ways in which your subordinates will express themselves and their emotions. They find it difficult, impossible, to divorce their sentiments from what could be a highly practical, objective way of looking at situations and other people.

These emotions affect the workload of your group, the profits of your corporation, your own rise to the top. Try these thoughts on for size:

- In the 30,000 or so years that we've been on earth we've been in much the same physical shape that we're in now; we don't seem to have changed the basic, primitive emotions which led to tribal conflicts, fights over property, murder, and pillage. Emotionally, we go back a long, long time.
- As babies, we come into this world wanting everything for ourselves. We "rule the roost" when we're very young, ruthlessly getting our way much of the time. We're greedy for all we can get in attention, food, comfort.
- As kids we start a tendency toward trying to get control of someone, to dominate a situation or another person. As babies we started off on the mechanism ("me first"), and we stay that way through childhood and sometimes even adulthood (I'm going to win no matter who gets hurt).
- Adults can't forget their past. It's with them all the time in their unconscious. The more they suffered what they considered

defeats and humiliations as youngsters, the more they tend as adults to react unwittingly to situations which remind them of those long-ago crises and disappointments.

- Some adults are so hungry for affection which they did not get as children that they go to great lengths to "protect" themselves from further hurt by affecting lack of interest in anyone. They appear to be cold fish, caring little about others. Some are anxious people who fear that if they become emotionally involved with another person then that person will "control" them. Their extreme anxiety to protect themselves forces them to become power seekers of the first order. They're not indifferent, just fearful. They seek superiority of some kind so that they will be safe from the hurt which possible rejection by you or others would inflict on them.
- Did you know that some people develop stress reactions from doing work that is far too simple for their talents, reactions that are equally as damaging to their emotions as trying to do work that is far over their capabilities?
- When you see someone who has suffered a defeat in the office, such as losing a promotion or not getting a pay raise, or even being fired, you might be looking at a person who is trying to win by accepting defeat. How's that? It's a form of "I'll-hurt-you-by-letting-myself-get-hurt" unconscious hatred.
- Everyone, including *you*, has a hidden desire to be protected by an all-powerful person. This need for a protective "authority figure" goes back to your early kidlet days—to the time of all-powerful mother and father figures. You'll never completely outgrow that inner desire. Nor does anyone else. That's why bosses, managers, and executives hold the power they do. They are the all-powerful authority figures for many adults.
- If you hear of any of your subordinates having marital troubles, remember that wife-husband fights are among the most disruptive and bitter conflicts we human beings can whip up.
- How's your *empathy?* Try putting yourself in the other woman's shoes, in her situation, with her background, and how

you'd feel. Remember, she may be trying very hard to act as an adult but her childhood emotions may be tripping her up. Be patient and understanding.

- Everyone likes to be with his or her "own kind." It's part of the "Who-am-I?", problem of identity seeking. We pretty much stay in our own ethnic, religious, political, educational, and social areas, because of the reassurances we get from others who are "our own kind." We simply don't feel reassured when we're with someone who's "not like us at all."

- "Imagined problems" pop up all the time because many people suffer from lack of attention. They feel that they deserve more recognition, so they make mountains out of molehills. Real problems can be dealt with fairly easily, but imagined problems don't go away easily. The created problems are inflated by prestige seeking, comparison making, responsibility avoidance.

- In some of the worst cases the very people who demand a lot of your time and attention are the ones who won't give *you* any.

- Whenever an employee wants something, that employee will generate a little fear within herself or himself that he or she "won't get" whatever it is that is wanted. Fear is part of the price of wanting something.

- Our emotions force us to believe in certain ways, and the way we believe creates strong patterns of habit. Because we believe in those certain ways, we will see only what we want to see. We screen everything through these habit patterns.

- Some people seem to "collect aggression." They go on a spree every once in a while to get rid of it, on a drunk, to a football game, a tennis game, whatever. They simply have too much aggressive hostility at times, and they try to work it off in one way or another.

- Have you ever noticed how some people will tear themselves apart a lot faster than they'll tear another person apart? And how others do both equally well?

- No one meets frustration without counterattacking it by some method of aggression. If a coin machine keeps your coin and doesn't give you the candy bar, you'll pound the machine a time or two. How many times have you been frustrated *without* acting aggressively?

- In almost all cases you can motivate your subordinates to the extent that you keep them fully informed and have them participate in the early planning and the carrying out of projects. When they *feel* that they are sharing some of your authority for making decisions and are an accepted part of the group they're more motivated to work effectively.
- In your group comparative emotions will cause individuals sometimes to feel uncertain about themselves and to develop a strong sense of dependency on you as their manager.
- In some instances a subordinate who is burned off about something a spouse did will come to work and transfer that hostility to you. Instead of going home sore at you and taking it out on the spouse, the classic instance, the subordinate reverses the order.
- The more insecure people are, the harder they work to develop security in their jobs. Some of them are able to control this terrible anxiety about losing their jobs, but others never get out of the insidious grip of fear that they'll be fired . . . even to the day when they receive their Quarter Century Club pin for continuous employment.
- People aren't really *aware* of their emotions. They do things and wonder why they acted that way. Sometimes they're shocked at what they've done or said, not understanding that they were letting off steam from some inner tension that had built up in their unconscious.

All right. How do you deal with this fat catalog of emotions that make your subordinates do unpredictable things, act unreasonable, say things they don't mean? Keeping these thoughts in mind will be helpful.

1. Tell yourself that no one escapes the grip of primitive emotions. Absolutely no one.
2. Nearly all the people you know are fighting in one way or

another to achieve some childhood expectations that they or their parents demanded. It makes no difference that these expectations are out-of-date because of adulthood. They keep on trying unconsciously to achieve them. From this comes a broad range of self-hate that crops up in your group, forcing you to find ways to cope with it.

3. You learn to take people as they are, knowing that you can work with them but that you can't change them very much. They will not become what you want them to become, no matter how hard you try.

4. In everyone there is a type of inertia that makes it tough for him or her to get rolling fast and stay in motion. This, plus the usual frustration caused by just having to go to work, makes it difficult for you as a manager to make changes. If you do make changes you'll find it will take a long time. Some people and some things you can never change.

5. The competitiveness of our times pushes all of us away from one another. We resent what the other person is getting because we compare ourselves to her or him and find ourselves coming up a poor second. We can't get rid of this resentment and hundreds like it, so we're hostile to others much of the time.

6. All this submerged hostility, this deep anxiety, these patterns of self-defeat make it tough for you to manage people. You make it easier on yourself when you understand that *you* are responsible for very few of these inner emotions. They all had their roots in your subordinates many years before you came on the scene. You are merely the lightning antenna, authority figure, the mother superior, the whipping boy, the big shot, the stupid idiot, whatever.

In short, there is not much you can do to help people with their emotional problems except to be *aware* that your subordinates have them and, despite them, to find ways to use your people to get the group's work done.

If it takes a bit of flattery, a bit of trust and confidence, some little special treatment here and there . . . give what's needed!

If you have to hold a hand sympathetically and listen to a long story, do it!

If you have to be the authority figure and "discipline the child" in someone, do it!

What you'll find most valuable is helping your subordinates to spark their self-esteem, to build a better image of themselves. Reward them for good work and good contributions; get them involved and participating with the workload on their own.

No one said management would be easy. It isn't, because you have to manage more than people. You have to manage today's reactions to things that happened many years ago and were caused by people many of whom are dead and gone.

Ways in which you keep yourself from creating conflicts

Did I hear you say, "I've worked with people for years and I've never seen any of that emotional stuff"? Perhaps you're right. You didn't *see* it—but it was there. And it does affect you. How much do *you* affect the emotional levels of other people? How much conflict have you originated because you did not understand the role your subordinates' emotions, even those of your superiors, play in the business world?

If you want to go on and be that person at the top you must avoid conflicts which can put you in a bad light. Some conflicts seem to be unavoidable, but most of them can be sidestepped if your antennae are up and working when it comes to other people's emotions.

Genuine warmth and affection of the kind glorified in novels and movies some decades ago are in short supply these days in the business world. People who work in your group are not very deeply concerned with whether *you* make it to the top or not. They have their own wants and desires. Some of them covet *your job*. And why shouldn't they?

Some of your people may be deeply anxious about their security. They may fear that you'll fire them. This fear stimulates them to seek as much power over you as they can get, no matter how they have to go about it. They are sensitive to anything which jangles their sharp-edged nerves of insecurity. Naturally they overcompensate and become power-oriented themselves. They look for someone to take the blame for the defeats they imagine they have suffered.

They may work to find some way (without their being visibly involved) of making sure *you* take the blame for any failures the group produces. They may start a rumor-mill campaign against you, with the usual bum-rapping behind your back. Mainly they will do little to help you achieve your goals and will concentrate on doing just enough to stay on the job. They may go over your head, pretending that you "don't pay any attention to them," are "hard to get along with," and "don't seem to know what you're doing."

Fortunately your superiors are aware of this sort of thing. They're watching you to see how you handle it and basically to see if you can escape the pinchers of human conflict at the group level.

You can escape much of the human conflict (which could originate with you) if you do the following:

Maintain effective communications with all your people. Don't keep them in the dark. Bring them into your plans and discussions as often as possible. Supply them with memos. Hold group discussions whenever practical. Don't make all the decisions by yourself; allow your people to contribute their ideas and suggestions. *Use* their ideas and suggestions.

Conflict is part of our lives. We see it as an ingredient in the TV serials, in our movies, in our fiction, everywhere. It is in the daily newspapers, in headlines, domestically and internationally. You can't avoid all conflict, but you can prevent conflict around you from hurting you.

Keep your ears and eyes open, hear and see things which will tell you if conflict is brewing that will involve you. You can tell from the little nuances which your ears pick up and from what you see that things are awry and heading for conflict.

Then *do* something. When you feel a conflict is springing up between you and one other person, nip it in the bud as quickly as you can. No harsh words, no finger pointing. Have a discussion and let the other person do most of the talking. Find out what is bugging her or him and make arrangements then and there to dispel any illusions, wrong impressions, misunderstandings. Work to replace the hidden fear that prompts this near-conflict with a greater sense of understanding and confidence between the two of you.

Do that and you're doing a good job of managing.

The tragic side of human conflict in business

Unmanageable anger
Unreasonable fear of failure
Deep depression
Unforgiveness of others
Troubled minds
Sense of unworthiness
Loneliness amid people
Suspicious hostility

All these states of mind may rise to their sharpest level when a person arrives at the stage of asking, "What have I accomplished in my lifetime?"

This person, as an example of all of us, has come to the moment of reckoning. It is the day of self-judgment, and he (or she) finds himself guilty of wasting his life. He comes to see how much time he has squandered, how much time he has spent not liking himself or other people. He or she mourns for the "lost opportunities" he had, jobs he didn't go after, promotions he missed, investments he should have made, on and on.

This person senses more than he understands that he let himself drift downhill after he got out of high school or college. He didn't keep up his studies, open his mind to new ideas and concepts, learn new ways and methods. He or she did little to assure his own success other than drift along with what seemed to be the only tide in the business.

The depression that sets in at this stage is formidable. As this person's manager you will find yourself hard put to cope with it. This individual has seen his hopes vanish. He isn't going to go any further. He may under certain circumstances see you as the major culprit. You stand in his way. You are responsible for his defeat! Or so he thinks in his jumbled emotions.

If you feel that one of your subordinates is in this stage, and sense that this is going to create a conflict between the two of you, have a long talk together. Listening is still the first antidote. Find out:

1. What can you do to help?
2. Can you work together to reevaluate his or her goals in life?
3. Does he have a fantasy about moving to the top, or has he been misled by the "status-seeking" bug to the point where he overanticipated how far he could go in the business world?
4. What would he accept in the way of an alternative or two? Is there another job, another department, another way of handling his job, what?
5. What self-defeating habits has he been engaged in that kept him from moving higher up? What are his hostilities toward himself and others? How can these be brought out and examined in the light of cold reality instead of in the dark snakepit of self-pity?
6. How has he been condemning himself, and for what reasons? How can he turn things around a bit so that he does no more damage to his self-esteem?

Do you *have* to hold discussions like this?

No. You can let the guy and his problems go. You can fire him, transfer him, ignore him. But are you being the professional manager you want to be, the executive-in-training that you think you are, if you waste good human material because *you* are afraid to talk to a subordinate about the things that are depressing *him?*

You can face human conflict and help diminish it. You can even keep it from occurring. But you can never escape it completely as long as one other person on this earth is within seeing distance of you. Conflict is a major ingredient of human life. You must manage it as well as manage the people who both create it and participate in it.

How to sense the "why" of what is going on in peoples' minds

Have you ever worked any place where the employees *didn't* talk about the company and the people in it? There's no such situation.

Company gossip is as much a part of the business world as coffee breaks, bulletin boards, payroll deductions, and quitting times. You are most exposed to what people think about the company and about the people who make up the company when you're having lunch or an after-work cocktail with one or two of them. Then the little remarks pop out, the digs, the jests, the envies, the despisements, the frustrations, the jealousies. Almost any relaxed conversation will free an employee enough so that the thing or things that bother her or him most will come out in the conversation.

So what?

There are some specific conclusions *you* must make about what people think of top-management practices and of the persons who are in top management. I'll list them in what I feel is their order of importance:

1. No company operates in a vacuum. The "walls have ears." Every pair of eyes sees something, and there is a lot to see because the motion of people in offices and plants creates a goldfish-bowl condition. Some actions can be concealed by closing doors, but the fact that the doors are closed opens up specula-

tion. In short, every person is on constant display. That means *you*. You are not invisible, even if you often feel you are. The eyes and ears concentrate on *you* as much as on anyone else. Remember that. Remember it and use it in your *image building*. Use it to avoid your image *depreciation*.

2. What people *say* is valuable information to you. Don't pass it off as chatter or nonsense. You're not the only one who can put two and two together and give five. Some people in lowly positions possess a keen talent for observation. Others jumble what they see and hear by a peculiar emotional process and manage to misunderstand it all. In any case, what people *say* about your company and its executives is part of your intelligence-gathering program—a rich source of data that indicates areas to be avoided, areas where you can contribute, areas where you can be successful. Don't pry, just listen. Analyze what you hear coolly and dispassionately. The grapevine can bear good fruit for you. The messages are there for you to decode and understand.

3. What people say is never as important as *why* they feel the way they do. The emotional impact of working conditions and of constant body contact with persons in authority creates either enthusiasm or stress in an employee. Do your people reflect, in what they say, a hidden bit of optimism? Do they reflect a sense of impending trouble, of crises, of deep disenchantment? It is important for *you* to try and sense the emotional levels behind their comments. It is almost like putting your finger on the pulse of the corporate body. You can feel a strong heartbeat or you can divine the growing illness within the giant.

Remember the old saw that as long as soldiers are bitching their heads off everything is fine in the unit, but look out when they stop bitching? Something along that line is true of business organizations. When employees vent their emotions in what they *say,* no matter how carefully they couch their words, they're doing the normal, natural human thing. When they clam up, then, indeed, something *is* very wrong.

What this all means to you is simple. Understand the process.

Don't be misled by the carping and small-time knifing. They are merely a safety valve that allows everyone from top to bottom to let loose some emotional steam. Part of your responsibility of management is to keep yourself a notch above the human tendency to criticize and complain.

Keep your antenna turned on, and *think*. Try to sense the *why* of what is going on in peoples' minds. Put this knowledge to work for you. Having your finger on the pulse enables you to rise faster in your management ascendancy.

You're not exactly a one-person CIA, but you're an important listening post. Knowing something about the reservoir of raw human emotions in your organization is a valuable asset to you. Your ability to piece together tidbits of information, facts, and fancy will grow over the years. It's amazing what you hear if you just listen and *think* about what you've heard.

CHAPTER SIX

Moving Yourself along by Mastering Others

No one really thinks of herself or himself as a "master of other people." That sounds like something out of the Roman slave galley days. We're a nation of free people, living in a free economy. We're able to do many things without asking permission from anyone. No one wants a "master."

In spite of this, you as a manager *are* in a lifelong type of training to master people and their individual emotional peculiarities and skills so that you can achieve the objectives of your group. It is a training which will strengthen your abilities to concentrate on management activities.

Management is basically finding ways to solve unanticipated problems and to smooth out the human-created problems while keeping the work patterns in effective operation. The training involved in "mastering other people" is a primary responsibility of yours. You're the major winner in this training, although each employee will gain quite a bit as well. It also provides you with another opportunity to assess your own managerial acumen and your personal characteristics to see if *they* are developing as you move along.

Establishing better inward information–getting ideas, viewpoints, contributions from others

In today's business climate, "profit centers" have become very important. They are a means of giving a management team almost complete responsibility for the profit, or loss, of a division, department, or section of a corporation.

A management team (that's your group) plays an important role in any corporation. It has a proven history of getting things done, of delegating responsibility to specific people, of bringing people with different but compatible skills together to do the work, and of establishing a method of clear-cut control over the various elements of a corporation.

The constant danger to a corporation is that old-fashioned bureaucracy will slow down the work process, jam up the communications, and make things more confusing. That's why good managers must be people who know how to manage, who can overcome obstacles, who can master the people in their groups with problem-solving actions.

"Management is a profession," an executive told me. "No doubt about it. Effective management in a corporation is one of the most essential ingredients for its success. The corporation is here to stay, and in the way it is structured to replenish itself and grow and expand it is as living as any part of the American way of life." How better could you say it?

One of the best ways for you to manage your subordinates is to set up a system (if you already haven't) of getting information *from* them. What you want to achieve involves:

1. Their original ideas, which can save you time and make more profits for the corporation

2. Their viewpoints on the work to be done, so that it can be better evaluated as to priority
3. Their contributions in establishing new business methods and new technological advancements
4. Their cooperation in meeting needs and opportunities as they come along
5. Their efforts to overcome human inertia so that they won't become bored with their job and will sustain their enthusiasm for getting the work done
6. Their participation in quickly solving "things that go wrong" without finger pointing for blame and without the inflexible attitude that "it shouldn't have happened in the first place"

How can communications *to you* help you achieve these objectives? Let's take a look:

Conversation. By having frequent conversations with each of your subordinates you have the chance to *listen* to them. You show your interest in them by engaging in two-way conversation. They have an opportunity to persuade you to their line of reasoning on various subjects. In a relaxed atmosphere, guided conversation can be the main avenue by which your people get their ideas, concepts, viewpoints, and contributions of original thinking across to you. Decisions can be reached, alternatives can be considered, participation in the solution can be worked out.

Memorandums. Your subordinates should feel free to send you a memo on any subject they feel will help you in your management tasks. The act of putting their ideas and comments on paper gives them a meaningful sense of participation. Make it clear to them, however, that they can't flood you with paper dealing with trivial items.

Position papers. These are general statements which you prepare and distribute to your people. You ask them to read them, think about the subject, and give you their reactions in writing. The subjects cover areas of information which are of top interest to you; you gain the participation of your people by spelling out the problem, its ramifications, its history, and possible developments or solutions. Used only when there is a significant situation on hand, the position paper can do quite a bit to unite your people and bring out their inspirational ideas.

Whatever system you use you gain immeasurably as a manager when you set up an inward flow of information, ideas, suggestions, viewpoints, and concepts from your subordinates—not on a one-shot deal but as a normal, accepted part of your everyday work.

Doing a better job of using your outward information facilities

Many managers prefer one-way communication because they feel it is easier just to instruct. It doesn't work that way.

Good communication is a trade-off. You may communicate to your people, but if you don't get appropriate feedback from them in an inward flow of information you never know how well or badly you're doing.

Effective communication on your part requires some effort by you, effort and planning. The purpose of communicating to your people is to motivate them to *do* something, or to influence them to *stop* doing something.

Use personal conversations (the best way), memos, meetings and position papers to sell your ideas to your subordinates. But don't be heavy-handed.

1. Give them the message concisely and clearly. Don't waste words.

2. Spell out the main points in easily understandable language.

3. Be timely. Get your communications out to them while the subject is still fresh. Make certain that your subordinates hear it from you *first* before they find out about it from some other department.

4. Use conversational language in your communications. So many memos and papers are dry as dust. Put a little imagination into yours and they'll sell better for you.

5. In meetings, do more listening than talking. State the reason for the meeting, what you want the objectives to be, how they can participate in working on the problem—then listen. Ask questions of the subordinates, such as, "Do you have anything to add to that?" or "How do you feel about what we've discussed so far?" Don't let them sit there and *not* contribute something. Bring them out of themselves, but do it easily, without any stress or strain.

6. In reports, tell them what the problem was originally, what efforts were made to solve it, and what finally did the job. Reports serve as a follow-up to show everyone in your group that problems *can* be solved and sticky situations *can* be gotten out of. Too often managers fail to report back and tell their people that things did work out rather well after all. The employees have a right to know. They'll feel more a part of your plans if you keep them informed.

All the ideas you carry in your head for getting your group's work done effectively won't do you much good unless you can put them across to your subordinates. Selling your ideas to them is one of your continual jobs. First, they *expect* you to come to them with ideas and programs. Second, they feel it's *your* responsibility to come up with the initial batch of ideas for a project. Third, they can be sold on the ideas and on helping you carry them out if you include them in the decision-making process. Accepting their advice on the ideas presented to them isn't diluting your managerial position. It is strengthening it.

Some experts say that one of the major problems in all business is the lack of communications. Others say you can do too much communicating to your subordinates. Which do you want, no communication at all or too much? Can there be too much?

What it boils down to is judicious use of the inward and outward flow patterns of communications. It means the use of *powerful* communications, particularly in outward messages.

What are *powerful communications?* They are short and meaty, say what you mean, prevent any misinterpretation of what you say, are frequent, and are aimed at being *understood* by your people.

Goal setting—how to make high standards important to everyone

"If you can get to the deep emotional feelings of your subordinates, you can make them enthusiastic partners in your efforts to reach the goals of your group." This is a statement by a senior vice president of a large electric-appliance manufacturing company.

You know that the only way you can win the complete cooperation of your people in achieving your goals is to bring them in at the "goal-setting time." Their attitude toward the goals is all important. If they feel they can participate in setting the goals as well as in carrying out the work designed to achieve the goals they'll do more.

It is obvious to all managers that goals are reached more easily when work standards to win those goals are maintained at a high level. That's the problem—maintaining them. You do it this way:

1. You set the example. Nothing will work unless you are free from criticism that *you* don't have high personal work standards.

2. You talk individually to each of your subordinates and explain what the standards are, why they are high, and what each of them can expect in the way of rewards. Promising rewards is touchy. It could be "group recognition," improvement in working conditions, more money for pay raises, whatever. You know how far you can commit yourself.

3. You monitor the work performance. When you see someone who is doing work that does not meet the high standards, call the person in right away for an intimate but low-pressure discussion. What's wrong? What are the problems? Why can't the standards be kept? Get at the cause of the problem, and help the employee get back on the right track.

4. No one can work at top speed or with a high enthusiasm every day for a long period of time. There are highs and lows.

Expect the lows and be patient. If there are too many lows and not enough highs in the work performance, start talking about it to the employees. Find out what is wrong. You can't take chances.

5. Remember, high work standards do appeal to many subordinates as a matter of pride in individual achievement. Take advantage of this fact by encouraging this emotion.

You're the example—show them how they can follow you

We have mentioned how *you* are the example for establishing high standards of work for your subordinates.

This is true in establishing positive attitudes which include not only maintenance of high work standards but also high participation in everything your group does.

You (it always comes back to you!) are responsible for creating the positive attitudes. Remember these facts:

1. You are on show every minute of the day. Everything you do is apparent to your people. If you strive for top professional performance, they know it. If you slack off, they know that, too. You are the sparkplug. It all starts with you.

2. You can encourage the positive attitude by playing down the negative feelings of your people. ("Too much work! Why should we do all the work around here? What do we get out of it?") Stress how it is easier to think positive, to shoot for higher standards, to win greater acceptance from the top brass. Emphasize that when your group wins the individuals win as well.

The advantages of listening to what they're trying to tell you

How can people get through to you with their ideas and suggestions if you don't listen to them?

It is case-proven that a great many managers and executives *do not listen effectively to their subordinates.* For some reason, all the way through the university and in their years on the job, many received no training in the art of listening. They were trained to talk, to act effectively, but not to listen.

Are you a good listener? Actually, or do you just *think* you are one? Here's a checklist:

1. I'm mentally *prepared* to listen to anyone who telephones me, enters my office, or approaches me outside the office.

2. I'm prepared because I realize that personal conversation is the *best way* to find out what the other person is really thinking.

3. When I listen I deliberately keep my mouth closed and my ears open. My sensitivity is at a peak as I look at the person's face (which tells me how sincere he or she is) and listen to her words (which tell me how concerned she is with getting her message across to me).

4. I will form no nervous barrier to the conversation by fidgeting, moving around, toying with a pencil, acting uninterested. I will show my interest by concentrating on what the other person is saying.

5. If I am in a meeting I will caution myself to be courteous to each speaker, make notes of the important parts of each statement, ask questions when I don't feel I've fully understood the message. In general I will show everyone that I am listening and that I am paying attention to what is being said.

6. If I disagree with what is being said, I will say that I disagree with the statement but *not* with the right of the speaker to make it. In other words, I'll never criticize anyone for saying what he or she believes to be important, even though I don't accept what they have said.

If you're willing to listen, you're going to hear many things that will help you manage better.

Mistakes and how they help you move ahead with your subordinates

Have you ever met anyone who didn't make mistakes? No. You've met people who wouldn't *admit* they made mistakes.

Your subordinates *will* make mistakes, some of them real beauties. Regardless of the situation, here is what *you* should do to take advantage of each mistake so that you and your subordinates will move ahead, with you as the biggest winner:

1. Expect mistakes. Don't be upset when they arrive.
2. Fight the temptation to be vastly irritated and to say something like, "What the hell were you trying to do?" Or the old standby, "What in the world were you *thinking* of?" You'll get nowhere with bitter remarks and recriminations.
3. Ask the employee what has been learned from the mistake, and set up safeguards to prevent the same mistake from being made again.
4. Show the subordinate that mistakes aren't the end of the world, just a touchy part of it. It is your job to convince him that "everyone can learn from mistakes" and that you have confidence that he *has* learned from his goof.
5. Give each mistake maker a definite course to follow to prevent further mistakes—if that employee doesn't come up with a course of her own. You want to develop learners, not to inhibit your people.

When your subordinates understand that you don't flip your lid over their mistakes, they'll try harder not to make any. And when they do goof, they'll look for the "lesson to be learned." That is what helps move *you* ahead.

You're the coach—train them in better work habits

Not everyone you hire will have the exact experience you want. Nor will all your present employees have the skills and abilities you need. On top of that, changes in techniques and systems come along from top management, and this creates the problem of training everyone in the new practices.

You're the coach. It's up to you to develop the type of training which will create better work habits either for the old workload or for the new systems. For the new systems:

1. Break the systems down into easily understandable functions.

2. Put it all down on paper.

3. Have a series of meetings with your staff to go over the functions. Who does what? What changes are in effect? What authority has shifted or changed? And *why* are these different work habits being instituted?

For the old systems, for which you want to pep up the sagging work habits of your staff:

1. Set up a quarterly review of work practices.

2. Keep the review to an hour or less.

3. Put your major points clearly and concisely on paper.

4. Have all your people contribute their ideas on how work habits can be improved, with emphasis on *why* they should be improved. Make certain everyone understands the reasons for jacking up work habits and what will happen if better work habits aren't forthcoming.

Effecting change—helping them learn new ways, new techniques

Resistance to change is well known. Most of us want to come to work and have the comforting knowledge that we can do pretty much the same thing today that we did yesterday. That's how poor work habits get started. It's also how boredom and disenchantment set in.

While you may be change-oriented, how much so are your staff members? You can do these things:

1. Talk up change. Make talk of change part of your regular conversational messages. Create an atmosphere of acceptance to change. Make your people aware that change may come at any time, that it has been thought out by top management and has specific purposes.

2. Stress the benefits of the changes to the staff members. Improvements in working conditions. Greater recognition for

their adaptibility to accept the changes and put them into effective operation.

3. Ask everyone's opinion of the changes and what might be done to smooth the transition from the old to the new methods.

By working constantly to fight resistance to change and by talking up change every once in a while you pave the way for your better acceptance by your subordinates of new ways and new techniques.

Emphasizing enterprise—creating an enterprising team spirit

Very few persons are what you'd call "enterprising," and almost no one likes to consider himself or herself as part of a "team" at the office. In light of this, your task of creating an enterprising team spirit within your subordinates is considerable. First, here are the reasons why you should try:

1. If you can make them into a more enterprising team you benefit because the group's work will improve. You'll make a far better appearance as a manager because you *have* succeeded in managing your people to do more and better-quality work.

2. There is a reservoir of enterprise in most people. It has been unused because there has been no demand for it. You can take advantage of this fact by making a demand on it. You'll be surprised at the response.

Second, *how* you do persuade your people to become "more enterprising?"

1. You establish a competitive spirit at the start. In a meeting with your people tell them you are out to beat another group or another company—whatever a good competitor would be. Tell them you are placing a special emphasis on each person's ability to help find new and better ways to do old things, to spot profit leaks, clear up bad work habits, and the like.

2. Now they have something to compare themselves with—not just a vague idea that they're "supposed to do better." Work with

them individually to stress that you need their creative ideas. Can some forms be eliminated, combined, made more effective? Can some work routines be speeded up and made more effective with less work? Is the office arrangement efficient? Is new equipment needed? What else needs to be done? Tackle the small problems as fast as you can get to them.

3. Show each person how he or she *gains*. They naturally are interested in "what's in it for me," and you must consider this aspect carefully. You can't bribe them, but if you can show them how the entire group will rise in popularity, esteem, and professionalism, they'll see how they will gain as well. Stress how group efficiency can be vastly improved when everyone contributes his original ideas.

4. Compliment them on their loyalty to the group and the corporation. Everyone likes to be identified with a winning cause. You can show them that an enterprising team isn't a one-time deal but a life-style. The team wins because it is on the ball. The corporation wins when it has many enterprising teams within its confines.

5. Stress the future. The corporation will be around for a long time. It needs men and women to promote. Who will get those promotions? The people who have demonstrated that they can contribute to the success of an enterprising team.

There is a bit of showmanship called for in "psyching" a team to be really enterprising. You'll have some resistance, because you're asking them to contribute more of themselves, more thought, more involvement. But people do like showmanship. They like the feeling that "we're going someplace."

How enterprising your team becomes depends, as you knew it would, on how enterprising *you* are in building your people up to it.

It can be done. Enterprising managers have proved this time and time again, and it has been one of their largest steps up toward an eventual executive position.

The self-help thrust—helping them to develop their managerial skills

Many managers shy away from helping subordinates acquire skills and interests in becoming managers. Why create competition? "They'll be after my job" is the normal reaction.

Reality tells you this: Someone is always after your job. You are always after someone else's job higher up. Nothing remains static for years. People move up and sideways and some move down. But there is always movement, which you can easily chart from year to year.

Reality also tells you this: You're better prepared to accept a nice fat promotion if you can show your superiors that you have trained one or more of your staff members in managerial skills. You have a ready-made person to promote into your vacancy —and from within.

You never hurt yourself (even though you're afraid you may) when you help a subordinate to develop his or her managerial skills. Don't expect much gratitude. People feel that whenever something good happens to them it was because they deserved it. If you go methodically about your task of stimulating your subordinates to develop some management perspective, you'll find them responsive because they *want* to receive special attention. They feel they've earned it, so they won't go far out of their way to show their appreciation.

Training them is the problem. You can try job rotation, you can assign them as short-term apprentices to learn specific skills, you can have them sit in with you from time to time in wrestling with the data-analysis and decision-making processes. Once you have picked the subordinates you feel have the flexibility and go-ahead power to assume more responsibility, then you must continue to give them more responsibilities to cope with. It is the coping process that makes managers out of employees.

You strengthen your group and you boost yourself when you keep a development program for managerial skills going at all times. And the people at the top will take notice.

Making committees work—the job of pulling everyone together

Committees are an unfortunate but inescapable part of our modern business world. A committee is named to tackle a specific subject. The idea is that "we need a number of minds working on this." The idea is so implanted in corporations today that they have permanent standing committees as well as the usual expediency-made ones.

Though you'll never be free of committees, you can do some things to make them more effective and less painful. Here are a few rules:

1. Don't form a committee unless you absolutely feel that it can accomplish its objectives better than *you* could by making a decision yourself. In other words, don't shove your responsibility onto a committee.

2. Pick your people for the committee carefully. Forget the hand sitters, arm crossers, and note-pad doodlers. Name the staff members who will stay alert and work on the specific problem.

3. Spell out precisely the authority the committee has and what exactly it is to consider, discuss, and make one or more decisions on. What types of alternatives are the committee members to develop?

4. Tell the members how much help they can get from you or other departments in the way of background data, information, opinions, and the like. You can't leave them blind; you must give them the information they need to help them make their decisions.

5. A three-person committee with one of the three named as chairperson is usually more effective that a larger committee.

6. Spell out the time limit. Make it specific. The members must

come back to you by such and such a time with their recommendations or at least with a report on what they've found.

7. Ride herd on them a bit about holding meetings and keeping the deadline in mind. Other than that, keep your hands off; let them do the work you assigned to them.

8. Keep in mind that committees *can* be extremely useful, but use them like tabasco sauce—very carefully.

9. Lastly, remember that effective committees which you manage make you look very good to top management. They know how difficult it is to form successful committees, and they appreciate a manager who can run them effectively and with usable results.

Promoting a successful subordinate to strengthen your organization

Most of us like to see some people get ahead, as long as their progress does not respresent a threat to our own security. When it comes to promoting subordinates, some managers shrink back. It's as if they were threatening their own security by building up that of a staff member.

The truth is that it must be done to strengthen the group and to strengthen the organization. Promoting good workers from within is still the finest way a corporation can help itself grow and prosper. For *you,* and your group, there are these points:

■ You've already had your eye on one or two outstanding employees, men and women who've shown promise.

■ You want to keep them in your group as long as you can. You know that sometime they'll move up to another group and bigger responsibility. Your job is to help them.

■ Always be prepared to tell your boss who is a likely candidate for promotion, who deserves a pay raise or other rewards. Nothing makes you look less like a manager than *not* appearing to know your people well enough to recommend them for advancement. This means you must maintain some sort of a personnel file on each of them, with notations as to their weaknesses and strengths.

- When you recommend someone, you are taking a chance that he or she will fail and you'll "look bad." In most cases, if you've done your work properly, your recommendation will speed another good man or woman on the way to a managerial job somewhere within the corporation. If you occasionally suggest someone who doesn't measure up, take it philosophically. Don't stop your efforts to promote good staff members. You're in effect promoting yourself each time.

Getting rid of the unfortunate human failures who come along

Very few people are total failures. Despite the tremendous outrages that harsh emotions commit within human beings, most people who take a job try to make a go of it. What we're talking about now are those unfortunate people who are so self-defeating, so filled with self-hatred, and so depression-prone that they are doomed never to make it anywhere.

One or two may make it into your group. Often they are "transferred" from one group to another as the other managers throw up their hands and stop trying. Some are able to con their way into a corporation, and it's your bad luck that they end up in your group. What do you do?

- Your job is to manage people.
- Your task is to manage problems and your workload so well that you'll move up the ladder and become a top executive.
- You need willing staff members to help you get the job done.
- You have no room in your budget for people who can't pull their share of the workload.
- Have no patience for anyone who has been given chance after chance and who flubs it.
- Call the "human failure" into your office for a confidential

chat. You know by now that he or she is *not* going to make it. Your job is to sever the human failure from your group in such a way that you do not provoke sharp sympathy in the others for the wretched person. You can get the others down on you for not being compassionate or understanding, for being "too harsh."

- In your talk with the failure stress that this is a tough decision, that he or she has had plenty of opportunities, that your group has a great deal of work to do and responsibility to shoulder. Ask the failure: "In the face of all this, what do *you* recommend that I do?"
- In nearly all cases, the human failures will fire themselves, because they have been lifetime-conditioned to think of failure, and here it is again. They'll accept it.
- Announce his or her resignation effective immediately with as bountiful a severance pay as possible.
- Display no personal animosity toward the failure. Say very little. What you do say must be sympathetic and reasonable.

Remember this, human failures do *not want* to fail. Their emotions are so gripping that there is not much they can do to escape and use whatever talents and skills they have. Such people are pitiful, all the more so because most of them receive a lot of help over the years from well-meaning people who want to straighten them up." All to no avail. The good work goes down the drain.

The human failures include the chronic alcoholic, the chronic absentee, the chronic liar, the procrastinator, the bumbler, the always-tardy individual, the sloppy dresser, the vulgar mouth, and you know the rest.

You don't need them in your group. Get rid of them as fast as you can once you are certain they are "human failures."

One last point: Sometimes by firing a failure you force him or her to do some self-analysis, a painful "Who-am-I-and-what-am-I-doing-to-myself?" examination. This could mean that he would try to get a job where his emotions could be brought more under control and where, at long last, he might settle down to becoming a human being with potentials rather than a human being riddled with a sense of failure.

It is not easy, this mastering of other people. There is one of you and there are so many of them. You never are completely sure of what is going on in them emotionally. All you can do is your very best, knowing that you'll win some and lose some. People are enormously complicated. You'll never get to know them fully.

It's tough, but it's one of the reasons your're being paid to manage. It's one of the reasons you're on your way to being an executive at the top, with a bigger salary and more prestige waiting there for you.

CHAPTER SEVEN

Picking up Speed by Polishing Your Executive Skills

One of the things you do *not* want to do is to limit yourself to a few capabilities.

Good executives (as you have witnessed) have broad backgrounds in many areas. They arrived where they are by picking up new skills, mastering different subjects, becoming aware of *all* the facets of management, not of just a few.

"I sought out the kind of people who were good for me, in the sense that they added to my growth as an executive," a vice president of a large men's clothing company told me candidly. "I sought out the type of business atmospheres where I felt challenged and where I could meet the kind of people who could help train me in positive thinking and in acquiring the right qualities of leadership."

This is what *you* must do in much the same way. A lot is demanded these days of top executives. To meet these demands you must come through the test of many different skills. In a sense it is a natural course for you to follow, this growth of capabilities. You want to lead, knowing that you'll achieve some power in leadership. Call it achievement, responsibility, authority, it's all the same thing —power.

"You can't grasp power and you can't hold power unless you firmly know what you're doing and where you're going," a president of a chain of restaurants told me during a chat on executive skills. "Your business acumen must include knowledge of how your corporation gains its revenues, what its total assets are, how it handles the sales of its products, how the market values of those products are established, and what the earnings after taxes are and why."

Your acumen must include a bit of looking ahead to the troublesome conflicts your corporation and this nation face. There are enormous problems that affect your business —pollution control, protection of the environment, inflation, price and wage controls, increased taxation from all governmental bodies, racism, radicalism, international threats to our security, on and on.

You don't operate in a vacuum. Business management is becoming more difficult and challenging each year. In picking up new skills you are influenced by these personal guidelines:

1. The more you know, the stronger is your professional poise.
2. With more knowledge you are more capable of dealing with problems of all types.
3. You develop more self-discipline for handling the work.
4. You learn to do more things right—the first time.
5. You learn to work easily with many other types of people.
6. You gain from an exchange of ideas with a greater number of different kinds of people.
7. You learn where to get help from others when it's important to do so.
8. You become more flexible, able to shift and change into effective but different work and thought patterns.
9. You become a better decision maker because you are faced with making more decisions.
10. You put your aggressive instincts more to work for yourself

and learn more about your capabilities through more achievements on your part.

Adding new skills is tough work. It means *you* must make the effort; *you* must find ways to get yourself involved in management activities outside or parallel to your present organization-chart responsibilities. *You* must volunteer for more work, and you must do the work. You know that it can be done, but being human you are a bit uneasy about venturing into areas where you feel you might not belong *right now* and where others hold the power.

Okay. Let yourself be stopped. Cop out. Don't add any new capabilities. Then where will you be when the big opportunity presents itself? How will top management select *you* when you do not have all of the background they feel you should have in order to hold down a bigger position?

Some day you'll face your own reckoning. When you ask yourself, "Where did my life go? What did I do with it? Why didn't I do more?" This day, sometime in the future, is inevitable for you. You'll not escape it because no intelligent person escapes it. Your answer to those heavy questions to be faced in the future will be better if you work *now* to add more executive skills.

Keep these points in mind:

"I want to keep on learning—it keeps me growing younger."

"I anticipate change—it would be a dull world without it."

"I hate status quo—it's a method of going nowhere."

"I like newness—it means growth and opportunities for me."

Let's examine some of the areas where you can acquire new executive skills or, if you already possess them, you can add polish to them.

You are always a salesperson

Your corporation is selling something. A line of products, a line of services. It's your job to sell, too. Sell your *enthusiasm* for the corporation and its products to the following:

1. Your subordinates. Keep them "hypoed up" about the good prospects of the corporation and *their* prospects.

2. Your superiors. Yes, sell your enthusiasm to them, too. They're often too close to the scene of action. They need to feel some of your enthusiasm.

3. Friends and acquaintances. They'll spread the word when they hear it often enough from you.

4. Competitors. Especially them! They'll be less sure of themselves and their company when they see how enthusiastic you are about yours.

As for competitors, find out all you can about what they're doing. Read about them in the newspapers and trade publications. Study their advertisements. Have a neighbor or friend write to them and get their literature, annual reports, and other printed information. Keep a sort of a running file on their progress and defeats.

I'm always surprised to find people in corporations who don't know who their competitors are, what they make, or how much of a danger they are. When you can talk knowledgeably about your competitors to your superiors you've made a good impression. That's for you!

Sell your ideas. One of our human mistakes is to have an idea, tell it to someone, and expect it to be warmly received. This is a natural trap we all fall into. People *do not* receive your ideas with the same intensity that you perceive them. They often must be *sold* or persuaded that the idea is workable and that they will benefit. Take pains to sell your ideas properly, and they'll produce more for you.

Sell your personality. You do this by remembering that you are on show every minute of the day. Someone is watching you and receiving impressions of you nearly all the time. You sell your personality by demonstrating your coolness under difficult conditions, your preparation for a project, your articulateness, your consideration of others and their problems, your background knowledge of the way things work, and your desire to move ahead on progressive activities.

Personality is something a lot of people lack because they make no effort to sell themselves. Sell yourself as someone who is pleasant, even enjoyable to be with, who has a sense of humor, who is not a grandstander, a loner, but who has sympathy and understanding for all people working for a living.

Personality is being yourself and letting it show through. It's the most sincere form of selling that you can do.

Sell your group. Show them that you appreciate the good work they're doing, that you have confidence in them, that you want them to win as individuals. Sell your group to your superiors. Tell your boss or bosses how hard your people work, how well they do, and what some of the highlight successes have been. If there have been some failures, show what you're doing to work with those individuals to help them and how you are doing this to improve your group's overall efficiency.

Don't take it for granted that your superiors automatically know everything about your group. Sell them on your good points and emphasize the special successes you've had.

How do you sell? Any competent salesperson will tell you this:

1. Know your product thoroughly, from all angles.

2. Know the advantages of the product. Why is it superior to another competitive product?

3. Be enthusiastic about what you're selling. Show that you have complete confidence in it and complete knowledge about it. Enthusiasm is contagious.

4. Sell as often as the opportunity presents itself. Being a consistent salesperson is important; one-shot attempts won't hold. You must keep selling over and over again to win the attention of your customers (subordinates, bosses, friends, competitors).

What don't you do? A good salesperson (that's you) never bum-raps the corporation or its products. Being waspish about the place where you work and the products that you sell is a ticket for Nowheresville.

Never overstate your case. Overselling is as bad as underselling. It bores a lot of people. A good sales message is brief, concise, simple to understand. There's no reason to beat a person to death with a sales message. Most people get the point fairly easily.

Never be unprepared. How can you sell anything effectively if you aren't ready to sell and don't have all the facts at your fingertips?

Don't kid yourself that *selling* isn't part of your responsibility. It is. Be the best salesperson you know how to be.

You are a purchasing agent

Purchasing, like the other skills we're discussing here, is not ordinarily your worry. But, as with the others, you still have a personal stake in it.

It's your responsibility to help the individual who is purchasing agent for your corporation. If you can help save money and time through effective purchasing practices, your corporation's profits will be helped. Top management notices things like that.

Here's a simple checklist of items, most of which you probably are familiar with, to help you work with your purchasing department:

1. Familiarize yourself with all the purchasing procedures.
2. Use the appropriate forms at all times.
3. Know what you want before you request anything. Can something less expensive do the job? Do you really need the equipment, forms, furniture, whatever? Don't oversell yourself on the need, but if you need it, what's the best you can get by with?
4. Discuss your objectives with the purchasing department people, so that they'll understand what you're trying to do and can offer their suggestions.
5. Avoid being "plush-minded" and trying to get expensive items which you feel add to your status.
6. Make your subordinates show why something should be purchased for them. You can't afford to be chintzy, because you

can improve morale by wise purchases of equipment and other items that are necessary.

7. Ask the purchasing agent for advice when you're not sure of a specific purchase—and take the advice. It's not your game; the agent knows it better than you do.

8. Watch your budget. Have someone in your group help you keep an eye on cost control of the purchases. Bad purchasing practices can be a profit leak for your group. You win when you prevent these leaks from starting in the first place.

If you don't know much about purchasing, go in and meet your purchasing agent and ask how it's all put together. How can you lose doing that?

You are a marketing manager

Why? A whole department filled with experts serves this function. Why should you become involved in marketing?

For a simple reason. Marketing is one of the most difficult functions of any corporation. Despite all the tools available, such as market research, market analysis, trend charting, and the like, the marketplace is usually such a changing animal that grabbing it firmly for any single moment is difficult. The more diversified your corporation is the more difficult is its marketing function.

You can help make yourself into a nonelected marketing manager by closely studying all the sales materials. Get yourself on the internal distribution list to receive all of it when it's made available.

If you see an area for marketing attention, suggest it to the marketing manager. Give all the facts, details, and reasons for your thinking. You'll probably find that the marketing manager has already been down that path, but you can't lose in bringing such suggestions to his or her attention. It will give you the opportunity to hear his or her story and find out what the objectives are. This makes you more alert for other opportunities to bring to the marketing manager's attention.

What is marketing?
- Knowing where your customers are located
- Knowing what they've been buying from you and why they are likely to continue buying
- Doing research to find out how you can extend some of your present markets and get into new ones
- Finding products and services to fill new markets
- Launching a new product and determining its success or further need of improvement and variation
- Finding out you should close down an older line that is facing a sharply declining market.

Like all areas of business, marketing has its own jargon. Sales forecasts, market planning, market analysis, market research are the easy words. The tough ones are market heterogeneity, product life cycle, considered purchase, creativity for impulse buying, etc.

Marketing is for the experts. You know that, but you realize that the more you understand about marketing the more you are adding a new skill to your storehouse of executive capabilities.

You are a manager of time

You have only so many hours a day.

How often has that statement come back to haunt you? Even when you roll out of bed, sometimes thinking optimistically, "A new day filled with new opportunity," it's possible to find yourself quickly back in the habit of using or wasting time.

Which habit do you have? Using time effectively is easy if you can control time. If you can, then you are able to achieve a great deal in a day's time and capitalize on the fresh new promise that each day holds for you. But often you can't control the number of interruptions, meetings, annoyances, and time wasters.

To build yourself further as a dynamic leader you must exert yourself to control your time. There is no other way.

In trying to control your time to make yourself more effective and to meet the expectations that top management has of you, you do the following:

1. Go after the most important things first early in the day and get them done or at least started on their way to completion.

2. This means you set hard priorities and stay with the top projects until they are completed.

3. You prevent yourself from being "fragmented" by having your secretary take your calls during the times when you want to be alone, or in a meeting, in order to get important work done. He or she can keep callers out of your office during the same periods and make a list for you to telephone or repay the calls when you're free.

4. Be decisive. When you're not, you'll waste time fiddling and being uncertain of yourself. You'll look for time-wasting excuses in order to avoid making a decision. *Make* the decision. Don't worry about making the wrong decision. Worry about making no decision at all.

5. Put a bit of a fire under your staff people. Stress how important time is without making it a continually unsettling point. When they see you organizing your time to be more effective they'll generally follow suit. If they see you goofing off or killing time, who's to blame them for doing the same thing? *You* set the pace by paying attention to time and not letting it get away.

6. Make yourself as organized as you can for each day's output of work. Being efficient is nothing more than being organized. Spend the last few minutes of each day charting the work for tomorrow. When you come to work, there is the blueprint on your desk, with the objectives written down and the planning all organized.

7. People are funny about time. Some don't mind wasting it at all. It's easier to be in a meeting, for example, than to be working in one's office. Be organized for the meetings that you conduct. When everyone is seated, tell them cordially that there is a definite time set for the meeting. Hand out sheets of paper with the agenda and objectives clearly stated. Have your secretary

come in and get you or ring you on the phone at the end of the time limit. You face the criticism of being "hooked on time," but your superiors will know what you're up to, and you'll win by having more productive meetings. As chairman of the meeting, keep the attention on the subjects and try to keep extraneous material out of the discussions. You won't always succeed, but keep trying. You'll win some and lose some, but you'll win more if you're really determined.

8. Preventing your staff people from delegating work *to you* might seem like a strange idea, but such delegation happens all the time—and *it wastes your time*. What happens is that a staff member will be buffaloed by a work assignment. He will keep it for an extraordinarily long period of time, then try to bounce it back to you with some remark that his "workload is too big" for him to handle it. When people do this, it's a cop out on their part; they lack the ability to cope with the assignment. Being human they won't take any blame; they'll attempt to delegate the work back to you, knowing that you might do it because of the pressing deadline. Your way out of this when you find it happening is to call the offenders in and stress the guide rules for accepting assignments. Remind them of the responsibility for completing them on time and that a job might be hanging in the balance. Theirs.

9. Give yourself a "security check." Think about where *you* might be hiding behind time-wasting procedures. Find them and stamp them out. They're hurting your rise as an up-and-coming-executive.

You are a manager of profits

"The name of the game is making money," the president of a manufacturing firm in New York State emphasized when I visited his office. "Anyone who doesn't believe this lives in some world other than the business world. I've been depressed by the number of managers who never seem to realize that *they* must help their corporations stay in business and grow—and make reasonable profits."

How do *you* help manage profits? Mainly by stopping profit leaks and senseless spending of money. Try these:

- Set priorities for spending; buy just the major necessary things, with no frills.
- Watch your overhead in terms of fixed costs and flexible costs; don't permit your budgets to get out of hand.
- Make certain you're getting your money's worth from outside services (where costs have been steadily rising) and from any internal services you're paying for. Don't take chances; investigate all costs.
- Keep an eye on indirect costs. How are you being charged for things over which you have little or no control? How can you control them?
- Are there better ways to improve your inventory handling and inventory turnover? How can you save money?
- What about your buying and leasing practices? Can they be done less expensively?
- Are your subordinates required to account directly to you for expenses and expeditures? Are you keeping watch on these items?

Give yourself a break in the name of profits. Establish clear goals of what you want to spend and what you want to save. Consider the cost of your staff, the overhead, and the money needed to keep you going as a group. Being economical doesn't mean you have to do without. It means you must *manage properly*.

You are a financial manager

Corporations run on money. Where does the money come from? From the sales of its products and services, from the sales of its assets, from interest on its investments, and from *borrowing* money.

Everything in a corporation comes down to money. No getting away from it. In your corporation study these points: Who controls the funds—a finance committee, the chairman of the board, the board of directors, who? How are they apportioned? Who makes the decisions? How are budgets prepared, and who approves them? Who makes the final decisions? How much goes into the employee profit sharing trust and other trusts? Who administers these trusts and foundations?

How much in debt is your corporation? To whom does it owe money? How has it arranged to pay off its short-and long-term debt? How was the money spent that was borrowed? Were favorable or unfavorable lending rates obtained? Did the money come from a bank, an insurance company, where?

Some corporations still believe in "paying as they go." They restrict their expenditures to fit closely with how much they anticipate they'll bring in during the year. They often have small amounts of profits left. Others believe in being heavily in debt at all times in order to have money to expand and grow, feeling that the interest they pay is worth what the debt gives them in advantages.

Your corporation's annual reports and quarterly statements will give you quite a bit of factual financial information. The proxy statement will give you more. The Form 10-K filed with the Securities and Exchange Commission is loaded with financial information. All this is available for your study.

You are a forecasting manager

Forecasting sales is one of the muddiest jobs in the business —muddy in the sense that the crystal ball is often cloudy. Leave forecasting to the experts because it takes long years of know-how for this element of the corporation to be effective.

Forecasting is a game of guessing where you're going, of peering into the dimly lighted future to see how well sales will be going six, nine, twelve, twenty-four, and forty-eight months from now. Most companies use an annual forecasting system plus a long-range one extending to five years. They use computers to help provide internal statistics on a monthly basis to check against their short-and long-range guesses.

They use industry figures, information from outside forecasters, government statistics, association figures, past performance records of their own and of their competitors—anthing they can get which will give them a clue.

In your area, if the forecasts are broken down to your group, you are left with the problem of making your own forecasts to double-check against your share of the total sales goal. You need the help of your key assistants in making certain you have a fair proportion allotted to you. You need to keep an eye on the monthly figures to see how well you are doing in comparison with the schedule worked out for you, particularly in light of any seasonal adjustments that need to be made.

Forecasting is tricky. Many corporations have perfected it and know fairly well where they're going in each product line. Others can't always be so sure because they serve turbulent markets that may change and twist. But, for you, look into forecasting and become acquainted with it.

You are a recruitment manager

All institutions die unless young men and women are brought in, trained in the old ways, and given an opportunity to change old ways for new and better ones. The need for "fresh blood" is obvious. Business "power blocks" tend to be concentrated in persons who are in the forty-to-sixty age bracket. They often get perilously clogged with senior citizens. They tend to do business in the same old way. Some of the top people become isolated from the realities of what is going on in the markets the corporation serves.

You can help strengthen your corporation as well as your group by bringing in as many talented young people as you have need for and can afford.

Fight the tendency on your part to be jealous of anyone

younger than you are. I've heard managers complain (weakly) that young people "are green," "don't know anthing," "can't contribute," "need a lot of training," "take a lot of time," and so on. *Nonsense.* That's pure jealousy and protectionism. You're above that sort of thing.

Keep your eyes open for "comers." Have your staff people serve as talent scouts for you. Refuse to do what some loggerhead managers do—hire "in their own image." You don't want people just like you, you want people who can bring fresh ideas and outlooks.

In all probability your corporation's recruitment program is tied to the bachelor's-master's-doctorate degree type of thinking. I'm not totally against that, but I do recommend that some young people who have *not* been to a university might be highly suitable for opening positions in your group. Look beyond college degrees, look for the "contributors," the doers, the thinkers.

You are a manager of meetings

I agree. There *are* too many meetings. They gobble up time, give you more work to do, stretch out your day into unpaid overtime, prevent you from doing some of your on-deadline work.

Nonetheless, the *purpose* of meetings is to present information, get information from the participants, discuss problems, arrive at decisions, obtain consensus agreements, motivate people, train people, and even inspire people. All that from *meetings?*

From good meetings, yes. Meetings that are just put on and not planned are usually a waste of time unless something happens to catch fire and make them worthwhile. The meetings *you* handle are opportunities to show what you can do in this human-relations area. You can do these things:

- Go into a meeting properly prepared. *Plan* what you want to achieve and have firm objectives in mind.
- Ask questions, speak up, and clear your mind. Don't be afraid of making a mistake in front of the others. The biggest

mistake is keeping silent when you have something to say or a question you want to ask. Contribute your ideas, suggestions, constructive criticisms.

- Make notes. You'll never remember all of it days and weeks later.
- Get everyone in the meeting involved. Ask them directly, one by one, how they feel about any proposed decision, what pros and cons they see on the various subjects.
- Dress up the meeting with visual aids, filmstrips, movies, show cards, documents, by using blackboard, flip charts, showmanship to help get your points across.
- Follow up with a conference report, and ride herd on the work assignments coming out of the meeting.

You know how some executives are "hard to reach." Meetings become excellent common grounds on which they can meet managers such as you and come closer to the realities of the business by hearing what you have to say. If you're running a meeting and one or more executives are sitting in, the best way to improve your lot in life at that moment is to have used this checklist:

1. Room arrangements for a projector and screen, tables and chairs, ashtrays, paper pads and pencils, blackboard, microphone, water carafes or coffee carafes, glasses and cups, etc.

2. Roster of attendance which includes only those persons most vitally affected by or interested in the topics of the meeting.

3. A theme for the meeting, based on the specific objectives you've set for the meeting. Under the theme comes the point-by-point agenda. You've alerted the other people who are to handle any of the points for discussion so that they'll come armed with backup materials.

4. You set a specific time limit for the meeting. You start it on time, run through the agenda in proper order, and end it on time.

5. Everyone participates in the meeting because you find ways to involve them. Don't let them sit unnoticed or uninvolved. Never!

6. Think ahead about the material you will prepare and distri-

bute at the meeting—what visual aids you'll use, what surprises you might introduce to enliven things.

Whatever the purpose of the meeting—to motivate people, to solve problems, to train people, to pick brains, to present new programs—make the meeting work by preparing in advance and running things on time, and by getting the full participation of everyone in the room.

There are too many meetings, granted, but each *one you run or sit in on is very important!*

Keep these points in mind:

- After the meeting is over, what will have happened that you wanted to happen?
- Are you convinced by the reactions of those present that you got your major points across?
- Are you able to determine whether you hit the people in the right emotional area in order to get and keep their interest?
- Did you put a little zip and color into your presentation, enough to showcase your major points?
- Did you pull your people together by getting them to identify with your main message?
- Did you show them how they would individually benefit from the decision or action you promoted?

Pardon the corn, but by *meeting* these points you'll pull off successful meetings.

You are a manager of communications

In corporations where there are no communications things often are in a bad shape. People hate working in a communications vacuum. They show their resentment through poor work habits.

Bad communications are better than none at all. Good communications make your work and the corporation's progress much easier. You are called on to be articulate in print and in voice as a communicator. It's never easy and it takes time, but it is part of your job.

Your means of communication include:
- Letters, interoffice memos, circularized reports, competitive analyses, management memos, and the like
- Use of bulletin boards, printed circulars, etc.
- Meetings, in which you can take advantage of the close attention of your people to talk to them directly and answer their questions
- Upward, outward, and downward types of communications
- Your share in the advertising program
- Your share in the public relations program
- Specialized communications to customers, to the industry you serve

Part of the task of being a good communicator *is being a good collector of intelligence.* The more you know about things, the more able you are to communicate the specific messages which will help you, your group, and your corporation.

You are a manager of authority

This might surprise you. The point is that everyone likes to have a little bit of authority. Everyone likes to have a piece of the action. You share some of your authority every time you delegate an assignment to one of your staff members.

It is amazing how even secretaries warm up when they can have even a small piece of authority, some of the responsibility, some of the action. They actually will do better work, although I've seen one or two become "untouchable" or haughty when their bosses gave them too much authority.

Delegating authority is something you've heard about ever since you decided the business world was for you. You were told you could get very little done by yourself, that you needed other people, that you were the manager and they were the workers—so, you had to delegate work to them. It's all true, as you've learned. What may be bothering you are these questions:

1. How far do I go in delegating authority?
2. How do I control people to whom I've delegated work?

3. How do I keep them from taking advantage of me?
4. Who on my staff is capable of accepting delegated authority?

As with so many other managers' responsibilities, only you can tell how far you can go in delegating authority. The best rule for you is not to be too cautious about it. Get the work out in the hands of your subordinates and give them as much authority as you feel they need in order to get the job done. Don't waive your rights to pull things back into your hands if you feel all is not going well.

Controlling people is not as difficult as you think it is. Many managers dread facing a subordinate and checking on a work assignment. If it has to be done, *do it*. You control people, not in the sense of a prison guard, but as an individual who keeps cool, wants to get the work done professionally, backs up subordinates by delegating enough authority, is sympathetic about coping with problems that are encountered but is firm in asking that the projects be pursued and completed on time with the desired results.

You can head off trouble if you delegate work properly and keep an eye on the progress or spot the lack of progress. Your job is to get things done. If your subordinates aren't handling a project properly you must step in and straighten out the situation, even going so far as to pull in fresh people to take over if necessary.

As for having people take advantage of you in your delegating of authority, you may expect some of them to do just this. What you do depends on your confidence in the person taking the advantage. If you feel it is an unusual situation, that the person is a doer and a comer, then you sit back and keep it cool. If it is a person you don't feel right about, and you regard it as a deliberate usurption of your authority, you stomp down. You call the offender in and state the rules in no uncertain terms. You pull the rug out from under him or her and keep authority away from them until they show they can be trusted again.

Authority is nothing to fool around with. Top management has entrusted a set amount of it with you. Keep that in mind. They want to make sure you conduct yourself properly with it. In turn, you must do the same. The buck stops with you. You are wary of delegating your authority to others if you feel it will set up a rivalry between some of your subordinates. You want to prevent conflicts of any type, so you choose your people well when you give them authority to carry out assignments and projects for you.

You had to earn the right to handle authority. Your subordinates face the same challenge. When they understand that clearly, your troubles of delegating authority are diminished somewhat.

You are a manager of accountability

Accountability is one of your strongest suits when it comes to creating an image for yourself in the minds of top management.

Are you accountable for your authority? That's the question they ask, which you must answer with your actions, not with your intentions.

You form an image as a leader to the extent that you tackle the big jobs first and get them done, set priorities for your staff members, have a knack for doing the right thing at the right time, and demonstrate your enthusiasm for solving problems.

You make certain that you gain credit for your good work by reporting upward to your superiors, sideways to your peers, and downward to your subordinates on the progress your group makes.

Just as inevitable as death and taxes is our being held accountable for what we do. A good accountability record means you're dependable and you're growing as a manager. It also means you've been picking up new skills and doing very well with them.

CHAPTER EIGHT

Zoom along by Tying It All Firmly Together

The vast majority of people in American business have "foot-and-yard vision" when they should have "mile vision."

Short vision happens occasionally to nearly all of us. A great many people remain in that state permanently. Short vision means we're engrossed in the pressure of daily events . . . minute by minute, hour by hour. Days flip by with maddening speed. Months drift off the calendar, and years fade away. And we become older without getting much further along toward the success we dreamed about.

Short vision results in delayed success. It means you'll go nowhere. Short vision can be a cop out. It means you may be unconsciously choosing to defeat yourself because unknowingly you *fear* success. You are "too busy" to worry about tomorrow or next year. You're too busy "surviving" in the rat race. You're so busy you're "climbing the walls" with all the work snapping at you.

The best way you can eliminate the disastrous effects

of short vision is by doing the obvious and extremely difficult thing. Tie things together by developing your own "mile vision."
Tying things together means:
- Making sense of *you,* as you are today
- Making sense of *your abilities* to succeed, to really make it
- Making sense of the art of *good management*
- Making sense of *other people* and the way they act
- Using your *strongest points* as often as possible
- Avoiding your *weaknesses,* which trip you up because you haven't as yet been able to iron them out

Let's take a look at the present state of your "mile vision."

What is really important to you?

Your short vision responds—a bigger pay check, a bigger title, more power, more prestige. Or so you say.

Your mile vision says something different. It says *what you really feel is important to you is your self-esteem, your sense of personal worth, and your sense of uniqueness.*

"You can't get away from your competitive nature, which makes you chase the buck, the comfort things of life, and the big hedge against insecurity," the head of one of *Fortune*'s 500 companies said during our conversation at an association meeting, "But what *really counts* is your self-respect as measured against how well you accept the challenge of your job, how professional you feel you've become in your work, and whether you've done something exepctionally good in your own eyes."

Psychiatrists would say that your short vision is your subjectiveness and your mile vision is your objectiveness. In the first, you want things *for* yourself. In the second, you want things *from* yourself. You're never happy just wanting things, even when you get them. You're never as happy with things (such as pay and titles) given to you by others as you are by *your own inward motivation, which you set up.*

The only real happiness and deep satisfaction you get out of life's work come when you have a motivation of your own choosing. A motivation of your own choosing, spurred on by disciplined controls that you put into effect because you want to, places you either in or close to the winner's circle every time.

In other words, what is important to you is not goals established by other people or rewards and incentives established by other people. What is of deep personal meaning to you is what *you* want out of life.

Clearing away the cobwebs of short vision

Many people have settled for less than they wanted out of life. They were brainwashed by parents, teachers, and the "system" into believing that they had to be in one or another career line of work.

Many a doctor would rather be a writer or an actor.
Many an actor would rather be a doctor.
Many a lawyer would rather be a professor.
Many a professor would rather be an ambassador.

Why is it an individual will often succeed in one endeavor and then cut herself or himself to pieces emotionally for not succeeding in something else? A fine engineer may want to be a fine golfer as well and not be able to break 100. A great financial expert may fail miserably as a public speaker, something he deeply wants to be.

Very few persons *know* with unshakable conviction and assurance exactly what they want to be and exactly how to go about achieving it. Even when some of them arrive at the place where they expected to "be" the person they dreamed about, they often find disappointment rather than happiness.

Part of this syndrome of "Who am ? Where am I going? How can I get there? Why am I doing work I don't want to be doing?" is caused by the mental blurs of short vision.

Knowing *what kind* of person you want to be is half the fight of life.

Knowing *how to become* the person you want to be is the other half.

When we're young we're influenced many times against our will. We do the things our parents want us to do. We do things we don't want to do because they're "the custom" or part of the "system." Our teachers are often relentless in making us conform, in preventing us from being ourselves and thinking and acting the way we want. The external pressures are on us not to be ourselves but to be like everyone else.

We simply can't find happiness being like everyone else.

That's when we develop a serious case of blurred short vision—when we get hammered into the shape someone else wants us to be molded in. We're so busy performing to someone else's specifications that we forget we are individuals with our own unique personality, we forget how much we savor the delight of using our skills the way we *want* to use them.

Conforming is a sticky cobweb. Doing what "is expected of me" only leads to depression and a bad taste for life. Following the herd leads you blindly into more cobwebs—the "everyone-else-is-doing-it" snare.

Make an effort *right now* to free yourself from external controls even if they go back to childhood days and are enormously difficult to wrench yourself free from. Make an effort *right now* to listen to your soul tell you about what it wants you to do with the remainder of your life.

The first step in developing "mile vision" is to see which part of the horizon of life you want to travel toward. You are the only one who knows what point on the horizon this might be. But if you keep looking at it long enough and hard enough you'll find yourself moving in that direction.

The management hurdles along the path—the bad side

Lumping the words "hurdles" and "paths" together sets a visual tone for this section.

In the business world you have many wonderful places on the distant horizon to which you can head. But along the path are many difficult hurdles. These hurdles are the *bad side* of management. As a manager on his way to become a top executive you find yourself climbing or leaping these obstacles:

Communication. Some employees just don't *listen* properly. At times they'll get your message clearly, and at other times they'll miss the most important part of it. You can never be too careful with communications to another person. If it *can* be misunderstood, then it *will* be misunderstood. You'll find yourself helpless from time to time in the face of this universal block to effective communications.

Personality. Despite your best efforts some of your subordinates won't want to stay in your group and under your control. They don't like your personality because it doesn't suit them to like it. One or more of these people may covet your job. They're jealous, and there is no way you can bring them around to your side.

Carelessness. How do you deal with people who do good work but who consistently are absent or arrive late for work? By their actions they're telling you they really don't want to work—something else is more important—or they "just can't get up" for a workday. It may have something to do with their reaction to you as a manager, but most likely they're only fighting themselves and you're an innocent bystander. Get rid of them if they don't heed your patient warnings.

You come second. Even third, after the families of these employees, because they do other work at the office. When they can, they work for themselves or for other people on your time and on your payroll. They'll even moonlight to pick up more money and then do their resting while "at work" for you. Don't warn them. Just get rid of them. They're business hustlers, and they'll never look at you through anything but the eyes of a confidence man or a bunco artist.

Authority haters. They're still getting back at the Old Man or the Old Lady. Any authority figure receives their hidden contempt. They may work with you for years, but you'll never get them moving at a good pace. They'll find a hundred ways to dilute your management effectiveness when it's aimed at them.

Corporations are dying. These pallbearers are sticking around for the funeral. They're disenchanted with the corporate life, and since they didn't invent it and don't control it they expect it to disintegrate before their very eyes. Every Monday when they reluctantly show up for work they're surprised to find the place still there.

I'm a minority. Almost anyone qualifies for the "I'm-being-discriminated-against" bit. People with this complaint are very touchy about protecting this special status because it's a good excuse for anything that ails them. There's no denying that all of us discriminate against someone, and that the minority people are just as guilty of the same thing in their own way.

Move over, Bub. Women are on the march. They charge that they work as hard as men and are paid less, receive fewer promotions, and are offered fewer executive positions. They're right. But beware of the few who want these things because they are women, not because they deserve them. Of course, the overall charge is correct—they haven't been treated as equal to men, and they are equal. The battle is getting hotter.

On the move. The illusion is that one-third of our nation moves every year because corporations want them to move to new jobs in other plants and cities. I'm convinced that the biggest share of this massive movement is by men and women who are seeking a job more acceptable to them, who become dissatisfied with any job they get, and keep on moving in the forlorn hope that they'll find heaven here on earth.

I want it now! The impatient university graduate who's heard those stories about $25,000-a-year salaries right off the bat and who wants to move out in a running start toward the top. These boneheads charge right at life, with a costly marriage and a hankering for a fast foreign car, a big house in the "right" suburb, country club membership, all that. Who will get the messy job of setting them straight?

The loner. This man or woman solemnly cut the tie with humanity years ago. No bridge can be built that will reach over to them. They don't need other people, and they hang around just to show everyone how unaware they are of them. They won't become involved with you and your goals.

Me first. A prevalent disease among Americans, "me first" results in rudeness, inconsiderate actions, and greater distance between people. The "me-first" bug bite may produce a mild itch or a convulsive fever. Almost no one escapes from it.

Guess who's leaving! You've got things going along well and the news comes that some of the top management persons whom you've been working with are leaving—fired, forced out, or leaping on their own. You're faced with the problem of coping with the replacement executives and calming your subordinates who are tuned to the rumor mills and have heard some hot ones—all wrong but very believable.

I don't have the authority. You're trying to get something done and you run into the brick wall of those people who are delighted to tell you and anyone else who will listen that they don't have any authority to assist you. You must see so and so, have such and such form, be there at a certain time, whatever. They love this act and relish every chance they have to pull it.

You're crowding me! We're aware that being crowded in big cities or even in smaller cities and suburbs can bring out our sharpest antagonisms for one another. People become quarrelsome, bitchy, picky, territorial-minded, depressed—and they bring their unpleasant feelings right onto the job.

Telephonitis. This is a minor vice, but it can be an irritating one when you have to stand by and wait for someone to finish one of his or her many personal telephone calls. You can warn them all you want, but they'll find a way to get to a phone somewhere. To them the telephone line is an umbilical cord switchboarding them back into the womb of some other place where they'd rather be.

You'll not grab me. Motivational programs bounce off these people. Even the best pension plan or profit sharing plan will have little appeal for these employees, many of whom are good workers but tend to be free spirits, not willing to be "trapped" by corporate lures.

The bad sides of management are all too clear. You've run into many of them and you have more waiting for you. Dealing with them *makes* you a manager. They are among your daily quota of problems to solve. Solving them requires flexibility, patience, and a sense of humor.

If you let them get you down, your "short vision" is tripping you. Your "mile vision" would show you that these are among the hurdles along the path, hurdles that you can get over when you keep your eyes on the finish line, not on the hurdle.

Management can be beautiful—the good side

We've just looked at the gloomy side of management. Though there are many sticky situations and "I-shoulda-stood-in-bed" days, management actually has many more good aspects than bad. We just concentrate more on the bad because it's human nature.

Some of the good things that will brighten your days include these:

Enthusiasm. How refreshing it is when your subordinates contribute this priceless ingredient to a day's work—when they're serious about getting their work done but with good humor.

No complaints. These beautiful people are mature adults. They are dependable, don't complain, handle their fair share of the workload, and refuse to be itchy or grouchy. They accept work and pay and corporate structure and feel they're being treated fairly.

Self-starters. These people have learned how to overcome the obstacles and to feel a sense of pleasure at their ability to take on and solve the really tough ones. Deadlines don't upset them. They, like you, enjoy the fun of getting things done.

Understanding. Your subordinates who listen to you and understand your goals and objectives are the building blocks for your successes. They overcome the communication roadblock and use their intelligence to contribute as much as they can to your programs.

Originality. Every once in a while someone will come up with a truly original idea, and you almost give a whoop of joy. Everyone has some degree of original thinking within him, but so few people use it. When someone does, it "makes your day" and helps solve a problem or two.

Humor. They used to tell funny stories all the time in the days when things were less busy and complicated. Today a good joke is hard to find, and yet (if you're lucky) some of your subordinates or bosses will occasionally take time to regale you with a good story. Humor is so essential to good living that it's a shame we Americans don't accept it more warmly in the business world and concentrate harder on taking advantage of it. There is nothing like a sense of good light-hearted humor to brighten a day and lighten the workload.

Pay raises. However your corporation is structured to provide for pay raises, it is one of your genuine pleasures to reward the good work of your subordinates by giving them pay raises. More money is not the answer to all an employee's problems, but a pay raise does confirm your faith in him or her—and helps that person's self-esteem.

The fun. There is real fun in working closely with people to accomplish difficult chores. We know that from our days with football teams, basketball teams, band and orchestra, theater groups, and other endeavors where teamwork is essential. I've always questioned the word "teamwork." It goes back to the days when horses pulled together in the harness. Americans are always individuals, and when they choose to work closely with one another, for whatever motivation, they sometimes give the appearance of teamwork. The fun is in actually trying to achieve this rare and delicate balance of human cooperation.

Getting to know you. Like the King of Siam, getting to know someone else from a different background, with different characteristics, concepts, education, and strengths and weaknesses, is part of the fascination of management. People are an unending source of drama, color, intrigue—more than you'll ever find in a novel, a movie, or a TV world premiere. Where people are, that's where the action is. Getting to know someone in a closer way is a cashless payoff of management and sometimes as important as cash itself.

I can help you. Though your main concern is helping yourself (if you don't, who will?), you're in a great position to help others. A good manager on the way to becoming a good executive does have *heart*. A good manager is considerate of others, tolerant of their weaknesses, and pleased at their strengths. She or he helps those who need help and expects nothing in return, because that is the way of a mature person.

Trouble spoting. Not all troubles come unannounced. Some of them can be spotted by your alert subordinates. Isn't it wonderful when you can *do* something to head off a possible trouble storm? This is one of the ideal situations of management, when you're not caught flat-footed by a serious problem. Instead, you've caught an early warning signal about its coming and you're prepared to cope with it. Heading off troubles through alertness is a true sweetness of management.

These are only a few of the good sides of management. When we view the management field calmly and dispassionately we are reminded that most people are good. That most situations can be dealt with coolly. That there are a great many more good sides than there are bad sides. If this were not so, we'd have to build many more hospitals to care for managers who couldn't cope with the strains and pressures.

Coping with competitive peers

Speaking of coping, how about *the other managers* along the way who are competing with you for the next promotion? A senior profit-center manager put it this way: "You can win or lose, depending on how well you're doing, and how badly they are doing, in building an image with the men at the top who make the decisions. If an opening develops, one of you probably will be chosen, unless there is a need to bring in someone from the outside."

Here are some of his pragmatic tips to help you cope with competition from your equals:

1. Don't take it as a purely *personal* competition. Fight the tendency to think someone is "out to get you." Think of it as a tough, unpredictable race in which the best person might not win. There's always that chance!

2. Work to make yourself the best person anyway. Don't lose ground by bum-rapping your competition; don't waste time worrying about what they're doing. Concentrate on making yourself look outstanding in the eyes of the race judges.

3. The judges of this race want to have a person who has demonstrated dependability, gets along with other people well, and gets the work done.

4. Don't let illusions distract you. You may think one of your competitors is extremely fleet-footed and has the eye of the judges. The actual time clock and the reality of the final wire may prove you wrong. In short, don't allow your negative imagination to let you lose the race before it's over.

5. Keep running. If this race does go to a competitor, bite the bullet, wish the winner well, study what you did that was wrong, and get ready for the next race. You can't expect to win *everything* in the business world, any more than the United States expects to win every Olympiad game. Stay in training, corny as that advice may sound, because you are *always* in a race for a promotion or a bigger job, whether you realize it or not.

The key is in not seeing yourself as you do but in *seeing yourself as the judges do*. You're doing the running; they're doing the watching, and they have the instant replay to study. If they decide on one of your competitors, it's because he or she managed to nose you out one way or another. Get busy and find out how this happened. Waste no time getting mad or feeling sorry for yourself. As the senior profit-center manager said, "Get ready for the next race, the one you'll be in better shape to win."

Dealing with the stereotypes

Competitors are one thing. You can respect them because they are *doing something* to get ahead. Stereotypes are something else. They concentrate on themselves, on becoming a character, more than on becoming a good hard-working subordinate or a serious competitor.

In every office there is a sort of central casting as in the movies, where you find your character actors. Such as these:

I was here before you. No matter where you go, someone was there before you. This person becomes a hater if you come in and get a job higher than the one he or she has. He'll take every opportunity to put you down by reminding you obliquely that he, indeed, was there before you. It never occurs to him that this makes no difference. He isn't going anywhere and you are. When you meet these characters, write them off. They can never forgive you for going somewhere when they're not.

About my kids. The most common character is the employee who has "the greatest kids in the world—let me tell you about them." You are forced to listen to the glorious accomplishments of the kids. They're so extra special! You conclude two things: Everyone has the greatest kids in the world, and parents who brag about their kids are in the purest sense trying to take full credit. "If my kids are that good, I must be even better," they are trying to say to you.

Please like me. Almost everyone indulges in *some* of this appeal effort. But some people are so uncertain of themselves that they *constantly* seek reassurance from you that you like them even a small bit. Here is a raw emotion and you can't afford to put salt on it. Do whatever necessary, perhaps just a friendly smile, to show these "please-like-me" people that you understand them and find them acceptable.

I love myself. Psychologists call them "narcissists." They dwell within themselves, and they're in your group only because they need the money to keep from starving to death. They may have talent and they may do good work, but they cover everything over with a thick coat of self-adoration. Dealing with them is difficult because they insist on telling you in many different ways how great they are. They're not great at all. Just their imagination about themselves.

I'm being picked on. This person is convinced that a grand conspiracy exists to make his or her life more difficult. "Being picked on" is a handy excuse for failures of all kinds. "How can I win if I'm being picked on all the time?" is a refrain stemming from childhood. It's an imaginary stone wall to hide behind. In some cases managers *do* pick on someone, but no one has to stay and take that kind of nonsense.

Wait'll I tell you. The office gossip proves one thing—he has big ears, a nasty mind, and an intelligence small enough to imagine the worst about everyone and everything. Trusting him is like leaving the keys in your car.

I'm here again. The office pest has all kinds of excuses to come into your office. He's hard to get rid of because he'd rather chew the fat than work. He knows that sitting in your office gives an illusion that he is working. He'd rather do that than be at his own desk working.

The workload is enormous. This is the chant of the Grade A, Class 1, Imperial Potentate Procrastinator who never can meet deadlines or get everything together all at once. Procrastinators complain constantly of being under intense pressure ("Who can work under conditions like this!"). They insist that they aren't the type who can "dash work off." They need lots of time to do a "professional" job (meaning time to put the work off day after day until it will be given to someone else for completion). Procrastinators are easy to understand. They have no confidence in their ability to do the work. They unconsciously try to delay any judgment on their efforts because they fear your criticism. If you criticize them, it only confirms their own poor judgment of themselves. You'll spend a lot of time trying to hurry this character, without much success. Unless you need him or her for specific reasons, say good-bye.

Ol' Stone Face. Somewhere, long ago, this person fell out of love with the human race. Nothing pleases him. Nothing moves him. Nothing involves him. He does his work in a cold, emotionless way. When you say, "Good morning," to him he may not even nod in recognition. Avoid him. Who needs a Mount Rushmore reject in the office?

You'll get the point. The friendly backstabbers are envious of your successes. They can't stand having anyone succeed other than themselves. They're very skilled at dropping little things into the rumor mills, at pretending they know something scandalous about you, at giving the impression you are covering up something. Backstabbers are hard to uncover because they do their work so well. Since the law prevents you from pounding them to a pulp (if you find out who they are), have a confidential talk with your superior and explain the situation. Protect yourself where it counts, at the top, not at the back.

Meeting new people successfully

You're "on show" everytime you meet someone new. Some people are colorful. Some are not. Some come on so strong they almost offend you; others are drab and self-contained. It is this strange mixture of characteristics that makes people interesting.

People try to live up to their self-images, and they often have a misshapen image which makes them do some of the damndest things to impress you and other people. They're basically trying to impress themselves when they meet you. They're saying to themselves, "Here is how I want to come across to this person." They act out the role they have in mind, usually one they've perfected over the years in the belief that they're achieving the image they want.

It is this "impression drive" which gives people their unique, characteristic appearance. It is this set mask behind which the real person hides. It is what they allow you to see of themselves.

How do you meet new people and see them as they are? You meet people, knowing that they are presenting an "image" to you, never the real person. There is no such thing as a perfectly calm person, only one who *appears* to be calm. There is no such thing as a perfectly cheerful person, only one who *appears* to be cheerful.

When you meet new people, be yourself as much as you can. Let *them* do the image pushing. Be courteous, pay attention to them, don't settle for firm decisions in your mind in classifying them one way or another, and show that you *are* interested in them.

When people meet, they know that they are on stage and they perform much the same as actors do. They do "what is expected of them." First impressions are often wrong. The key is not what people act out, nor what they say. The key is in what they *do*.

Pay more attention to the things they do, than to the camouflage. And check yourself to see how much camouflage *you* are using.

Handling misfits and troublemakers

There are relatively few misfits and troublemakers in American business. It could be your poor fortune to have one or more of them in your group. How do you handle them?

Misfits are near-tragic people. They often are capable of doing outstanding work, but they suffer such massive hang-ups that they can't tolerate "the system" for any length of time. A misfit is just what the name implies, a human being who does not fit into the close social circle of a management group. Such people do not attack the group or its individuals. They tend to avoid the group. They feel better when they are alone or in the company of another misfit or two, so that they can share their intolerance of "the system" with someone.

Misfits can't be handled in the normal sense. If one happens to have an unusual skill, perhaps that person can be kept on the job but isolated as much as possible from contact with the others in your group. Misfits have a habit of going their own way and doing things in their own time. Misfits are made so by a wrecking combination of self-hate and hate of authority. Their self-inflicted isolation is their attempt to lessen the pain of being with others and of being under the domination of a boss.

Troublemakers are always convinced they're being cheated by someone or by the corporation. "How come I'm not getting mine?" is their line. The troublemakers are always unhappy with something. "No one around here ever takes my advice," they'll say, or, "If I ever leave here the place will fall apart!"

Troublemakers are that way because they are impelled to draw attention to themselves. They discovered as children that people would pay attention to them if they "did something bad." Now, in later years and in the business world, they are sophisticated enough to "do something bad" in the very narrow spectrum of criticism and semichallenge.

Like the misfits, they often are capable of skilled work. Unlike the misfits, they don't want to be apart. They want to be in the middle of things, where they can make it clear that they're "getting the short end" and that "this is a cruddy place to work." They spread their acid of unhappiness to anyone who will listen. Usually they're found out for what they are, eternal gripers and bitchers and sharp tonguers, and their coworkers suffer them in silence.

In both cases it's up to you to decide how much you *need* them.

If they can do their jobs and not tear your group apart, you can keep them. But if you see evidence that their hang-ups are eating into the spirit of your group, move them out quickly.

Helping yourself with public speaking

One of the characteristics the brass at the top want in the individuals they promote into the executive suite is—articulateness. Anyone can run off at the mouth, and most of us do a bit of that from time to time. Being articulate means saying exactly what you mean in as few words as possible with the greatest amount of understanding on the part of the people the message is addressed to. It means getting your point across clearly.

Public speaking is one way to test yourself. Many people are afraid of appearing before a large group to give a formal talk. For most of them the fear is groundless. Anyone can give an effective speech as long as he or she knows the subject and is interested in telling other people about it.

Have you watched some of the on-the-street TV interview programs where the news side of the station wants to report public reaction to a big event? Attorneys, bus drivers, policemen, shoppers—all are articulate in answering the questions. Why? Because they have an opinion about the subject and don't mind saying so.

It's the same way with you. Find the subjects that interest you most. Either prepare an outline of the major points you want to make or write out the whole talk. Rehearse it at home until you have it down pat in your mind. You're ready for a public appearance.

Keep these things in mind:

1. Public speaking is not a natural function. Most people are anxious about it. They fear that they will not make a good appearance, that they'll do something that will embarrass them. So it is with you.

2. The public, on the other hand, is sitting there *wanting* to hear what you have to say. For them it is a mixture of education, information they can use, and entertainment. They like to hear other people's viewpoints and to hear something that might be meaningful to them. They are, in effect, friends. And unless you intend to stir them up with an attack on them, they will remain friendly to you as long as you don't talk overtime and repeat your major points to the verge of boredom.

3. Try never to speak more than fifteen or twenty minutes. Pep up your talk with language that puts your messages across and still instills a bit of color and humor into what you say.

The main thing about public speaking is that *you benefit* most. You earn the attention of the crowd. You get your messages across to them. They become more aware of you and your name. Your management learns that you *can* give a speech and are impressed with your ability.

It makes no matter if your are the only speaker before a crowd, one of several, a member of a panel, an interviewee on a TV program or a radio show. The thing that counts is that *you* can do your thing in public speaking and do it well. You are the biggest winner.

The critical shortage of well-rounded executives

In United States business there are a lot of executives. "Not all of them are good," an executive placement officer pointed out to me. "Not all of them are skilled enough to fill their jobs. Many of them are there under a sort of a truce because no one else was found who had better a background. There is a constant need for well-rounded managers who can move up to become naturally well-rounded executives."

What this means for you, despite what you might hear from your friends, is that there are many opportunities available for you in the executive echelon if you have the skills that are required. It's up to you.

Are you aiming high enough?

Most people don't.

"They seldom have a long-range plan working for them, so they're forced to make short-term decisions," the executive placement officer said. "They make their moves only when they're virtually forced by circumstances to do so."

With *you* it could be different. You know you have ability. You know you are capable of learning many more things. You know you can polish yourself into the type of functioning executive that is needed at the top.

The way to the top is not closed to you. You are the only one who can close off the route to the top. You are the one who decides if you're on the right path to reach the top. You are the one with the motivations that will take you there.

There's an old saying that "You are what you believe yourself to be." Faith, belief, trust, confidence—all in yourself and in your ability to make something out of your life. Aim high. By tying everything together you give yourself the kind of force-thrust which will help you reach your spot at the top.

CHAPTER NINE

Evaluating Your Progress at Checkpoints Alpha, Baker, Charlie

When you reach the Berlin Wall there is a gate named Checkpoint Charlie which has gained international fame. Persons going into or coming from Communist East Berlin go through Checkpoint Charlie. Before *you* move from managerial status to executive status *you* must also pass through checkpoints. Yours are Alpha, Baker, and Charlie.

At this time in your life it is essential that you review again who you are, where you are going, and what you are doing to get there. Self-examination of this sort is difficult. Who likes to pry into his or her emotions and motivations? Who likes to struggle with human conflicts? Who likes to face reality instead of hugging fantasies and illusions?

Yet, self-examination leading to greater self-knowledge is essential if you are going to achieve your goals. In the past chapters, we have done quite a bit of peering into you and looking at what makes you tick. Let's do it again but in a slightly different way in order to get ready for the main checkpoints.

A preliminary check on your basic emotions

What are your responses to these statements—affirmative or negative?

"I've been unhappy with what I've done with my life up to now."

"I find I've become filled with anxieties I can't quite understand."

"Frankly, I'm at the point where I'm discouraged and depressed."

"I feel tired quite a bit of the time. 'Fatigued' is a better word. I can't seem to get up either for work or for the family responsibilities."

"I seem to have psychosomatic problems as a result of the frustrations I feel about my job and my family."

"I haven't been able to get out of life the things I wanted—a better job, a bigger house, a better car, money for travel, money for my kids' education. I'm hurting and I need help."

Somewhere in that list you responded affirmatively. You saw some of yourself in each statement. You would be less than human if, after working some years for a living and striving to get ahead, you *didn't* feel some frustrations and some sense of inadequacy. You're not excused any more than other people from the same tangled emotions that make our lives so difficult.

The preliminary checklist of the strong, basic emotions that are involved in your progress toward an executive title include these:

1. *Anticipation*. I'm looking forward to having more authority, more money, more prestige, all that comes with a spot at the top.

2. *Enthusiasm*. I'm eager to use all the energy and skills I have to reach the top. I know I haven't reached my full potential for growth. I know I can do more complicated work and achieve greater results for my corporation.

3. *Acceptance*. I know that no one can guarantee to me that I'll reach the top. I'm willing to accept the roadblocks and hurdles as

a built-in part of the road to the top. Nothing personal, just part of the game. Everyone has his own share of conflicts and struggles with which to cope in trying to reach the executive suite.

4. *Conviction.* I'm at that stage in my life where I'm ready to devote a lot of my time to trying to achieve my major goals. I know I'm in a race with time and with others who want the same things. I'm convinced that I have the qualities to be effective at the top, and I want the chance to prove it.

5. *Dedication.* From this point on I'll quit *thinking* about doing something to help myself. I'll start *doing* the things I know I must do in order to get to the top. There is no substitute for solid action that shows how good I am as a manager and how well I would function as an executive.

With these emotions and their companions working for you, you can make considerable progress. A firm grip on your good basic emotions is the first step in controlling your destiny for the remainder of your life in the business world.

Realizing that you're the boss of yourself

"Controlling your destiny" sounds fine. *How* do you do it? You do it by studying the following points and relating them to your past life, your present life, and what might be in the future:

- *You* have caused nearly all your own major troubles.
- *You*, not external sources, are responsible for what has happened to you emotionally.
- *You* and no one else made the decision to be the kind of person you are today.
- *You* are the only one who can decide what you want to be tomorrow and in the years ahead.
- *You* are the guilty person who unconsciously sets up things so that someone will take advantage of you, humiliate you, beat you at Games People Play, make you feel second-class.

- *You* are the only person who can persuade *you* to rip the locks off the door to the inner room where you've stored your real abilities—so that these abilities can be put to work moving you up the ladder.
- *You* are the planner of your own fate—no one else.
- *You* are the one who decides to master your destiny and begin making the necessary changes, inward and outward, to achieve the goal you want.

You, in short, got yourself into whatever mess you're in, and *you can change yourself enough to get yourself out!*

I know hundreds of men and women who came to the same emotional crossroads where you now stand, who "took charge" of themselves, and went on to achieve their goals in life.

No one, absolutely no one, is stopping you from controlling your own destiny, from getting what you want out of life.

The terrible truth is that we all make our own troubles as adults. We do this for a weird variety of reasons, and we suffer when we don't work to free ourselves from these asinine childhood entanglements. When we do struggle to take control of our adult lives, it's amazing how much we can achieve. Doors we thought were closed forever are opened. Jobs we thought we'd never qualify for become ours. Responsibilities we thought would crush us we handle easily. The difference is: *We run our lives, we don't let our lives run us.*

Taking a look at what we mean by "goals"

The word "goals" is one of those catchalls which mean many things to different people. When we say "goals" in the business world, *on the surface we're saying that we want to rise to the top,* to "get the most out of ourselves," to "get more money and more influence," to "get as much as I can for my spouse and kids," and, the old standby, to "give me some security for when I'm older." These are extremely worthwhile, but they are *motivations* more than *goals* when you relate them to your actions *in the business world. The real goal you seek is to be your own person.*

"You want to stand on your own feet and be free and independent of others," a controller of a medium-sized Canadian metals company said. "You want the autonomy of being a proved manager and a proved executive. You want freedom from the neurotic distress you cause yourself when you lag behind, feeling sorry for yourself, blaming other people and situations for your lack of progress."

Your real goal is the mature enjoyment of your work and your love for those close to you. All else is secondary, no matter how much you prize a membership in a country club, a new sailboat, a new home, a trip to Europe, a fat bank account.

You know there are countless examples of people around the world who don't have all the goodies of life but who are supremely contented because they have achieved independence from others. Each is one's own person—and despite their humble existence these people walk in maturity and live with a dignity that many American businesspersons will never know.

For you to achieve your goal, that of being your own person you are faced with the task of rearranging your control of your emotions. You need to have your innermost self well under control, to have this strong control as the solid support on which you stand to meet the challenges and conflicts of life.

No one can cope with everything in life *without* freedom from unreasonable anxiety, *without* control of one's emotions through awareness of how those emotions work to one's detriment. You can master the conflicts that come along. You can be a masterful problem solver. You can make your own decisions of what to do and not do when you use the strength you receive from mature control of your basic emotions.

Your goal *can* be achieved. As we move through the remainder of this chapter you'll see how you can, indeed, make a fresh start toward your goal of being your own person.

Checkpoint ALPHA: understanding your boss

You win or lose to the extent that you impress your various bosses on the way up. A bad report on you from any one of your bosses can stymie you on your progress upward. A good report will help speed you on your way.

I've always been struck by how so many managers see their bosses as competitors, roadblocks, bores, nuisances, incompetents, dumbbells, phonies, or grouches. Some bosses may be one or more of these things, but as far as your progress to the top is concerned there is only one way to look at your present boss. The elements of that "clear look" are these:

1. Your immediate superior is in an excellent position to evaluate you, your managerial record, and your potential as an executive.

2. He or she is in a position to help you if you show that you will use the help to become a better manager.

3. Your boss's recommendation will carry weight when the time comes for a promotion for which you might be considered.

4. Your boss is in a fine spot to teach you more of the fine points of the corporation, of management, of human relations.

5. Your boss is no dummy. He or she came up the ladder the way you are. He knows something of your problems. He's impressed when he sees how you're working to get the job done through other people.

6. Your boss hears a lot more than you think. He or she has many sources of information. He is moved only by the truth of the situation, not by theatrical flourishes and fancy footwork.

Look at your boss as someone who can help you. He didn't make it to where he is by sitting on his duff. He did some of the right things. What were these things? What can you learn from him that will help you?

Point 1. Evaluating your service to your boss. You report to him, and he has supervision over you. How well do you help him carry out his programs to achieve his objectives? How much confidence does he have in your ability to accept greater responsibility? If he is to recommend you for promotion, what would be your main features that he would list in support of his recommendation?

It would all depend on how much service you have given him, on how much value these services are in his eyes. Have you helped him in these areas?

- Studied his responsibilities so that you know what it is he is supposed to do, what his goals are, and what his techniques are for trying to achieve those goals?
- Acquainted yourself with how your boss fits in with the rest of the executive echelon, who his boss is, how he reports to his own boss, and what his options are for moving further upward in the corporation?
- Looked for areas where you can offer assistance in the form of ideas, suggestions, opinions, facts and figures—information and viewpoints which will help him make his decisions?
- Carried out his assignments to you in good time, meeting his deadlines and accomplishing what he wanted done?
- Found areas which you believe he might have overlooked where troubles could begin and where early work can prevent the troubles from developing?

It is part of your job to be of service (without being asked) to your immediate superior. The more you work to help your boss, the more you can expect him to help you when the promotion and pay raise times come along.

Point 2. The problems your boss faces. In some ways, his problems are similar to yours. He wants to survive in the business world, he wants to achieve his personal goals and to help the corporation achieve *its* goals. Among the many problems he faces are these:
- Making effective decisions
- Finding the right individuals to get the work done
- Getting special assignments done on time

- Getting everyone to work cooperatively with the others
- Assuming full profit-center responsibility for his area
- Being accountable for all work done under his supervision
- Looking for places to which he can be promoted
- The need for accurate information from you on which he can base decisions and judgments
- The need for listening devices to help him sense the ways in which the corporate winds are blowing
- The need to keep his own emotions under control
- The desire to keep from being boxed in or booby-trapped by his own competitors
- The desire to gain approval by his superiors (up to and including the board of directors) for his good executiveship

Point 3. The human qualities of your boss. Employees tend to "give" a boss more glamour and power than he possesses. See how we glorify movie actors and politicians, ascribing to them qualities they don't actually have but which we "give" them anyway because of their position.

You should look beyond the title, the big office, and the other accouterments of the boss's job and see what his or her human qualities really are. A good boss (male or female) has some if not all of these human features:

- He is interested in the people who work for him, and he genuinely tries to help them within reasonable boundaries.
- He is determined to do all he can to help the corporation stay in business and prosper through normal growth.
- He keeps himself well informed about what the people under his control are doing, particularly the managers. (That means you.)
- He keeps abreast of what is going on in the market, in the industry, with competitors.
- He listens more than he talks. He wants input from his people.
- He is understanding of the human animal. He knows that good people have bad days and mediocre people have good days.

He is willing to forgive and forget if the total workload of an individual is good in spite of an occasional spotty performance.

- He knows that "job satisfaction" is vastly important to nearly everyone, and tries to contribute to the job enrichment of all his subordinates as much as he possibly can within the limits of his authority.
- He understands "the art of change" and knows that an organization that does not change, *that refuses to change,* is a dying organization. He welcomes progressive change.
- He brings dignity to the position by acting calmly and with disciplined control whenever "the heat is on." He refuses to blow his lid when things go wrong (and how they will do that!) or to look for someone to blame.
- A good boss is "some kind of person!"

Point 4. *What you should ask your boss to do for you.* Just because he is your boss doesn't mean he is isolated or some sort of god to be worshipped from afar. Put his knowledge to work for you. He is an extremely valuable counselor and guide, and should not resent your asking for assistance along the following lines:

- Check your major decisions with him from time to time.
- Tell him why you arrived at your decision, and ask if he sees something that you might have missed.
- Ask him for advice on any further studies you feel you should undertake . . . night school, seminars, reading of books, and the like. He will be able to steer you in the right direction and save you a lot of time you might waste stumbling around on your own.
- See how he feels about any unusual human conflicts that come up in your group. He may have had some experience in the same spot.
- When you feel the time is ripe, ask for suggestions as to what you can do to better yourself in the corporation. Does he think you're headed in the right direction? What can you do to serve him better?

■ When he gives you an assignment that has some sharp edges, spend enough time with him asking questions until you understand every facet of the task. He'll appreciate your concern about knowing exactly what he had in mind.

Bosses are human. They have many things to do and short days in which to do them. But they will take time to discuss matters of importance to you. Give your boss a chance to gauge what you're doing by having brief conferences from time to time, conferences that *you* ask for.

He won't resent your asking questions and asking if he will do things to help you. In fact, if you *don't* present yourself to him on logical questions, he'll begin to wonder what sort of a person you are. He could come to the wrong conclusion. Get in there at appropriate times and show him you need his help and are pleased to get it from him.

Checkpoint BAKER: how much are you helping the corporation?

We all give lip service to how much we're devoted to the corporation and how much we're striving to "help" it. How sincere are *you* in helping your corporation?

It depends on how well you understand the basic structure of the corporation and why we Americans have developed it to its present state. The corporation is a method by which hundreds, even many thousands, of people can work together for their mutual benefit. We all seem to labor under some illusions about corporations:

1. Top management runs the corporation. *Not true*. They try, but their authority goes only so deep. The vast majority of decisions are made by middle- and lower-level management people—including *you*.

2. The corporation makes people. *Not true*. People make the corporations.

3. Corporations are unchangeable. *Not true*. People change all the time in their group makeup, and as they do the corporations

change as well. No corporation today is what it was five, ten, and twenty years ago.

4. Corporations are extremely powerful. *Not true, completely.* There is a canard that "big business" dominates the government. This is just as true as "big labor," "big farm blocks," "big private interest," and "big national associations." What is true is that the *leaders* of big business, labor, farm groups, private interests (such as the oil people), and associations tend to try to influence government because they *represent* huge organizations.

Big corporations pay a lot of taxes. They have a lot of money to use in acquiring influence in government circles, and *they do use this influence.* But just as often, "big business" fails to dominate completely. Many times it falls on its face. Many times it influences the wrong people. Many times it exhibits incredibly stupid misconcepts of how things are.

5. People are swallowed up by corporations. *Not true.* People are dominated only if they allow themselves to be. Even the lowliest clerk can find ways to make the corporation his servant—perhaps in the tiniest way, but surely in some way. The illusion created by those big buildings and those complicated organizational charts makes many of us believe that people *are* swallowed up. The truth is that *people* run the corporations, and people use the buildings, the offices, the desks, and the day's labor to provide protection for themselves. Without those buildings and things to do what would happen to the people? No. People keep the corporations going because of the security that they provide.

Now back to you. Here is a checklist of *positive thoughts* which are of the type to help you find ways to help your corporation:

1. I realize that the people at the top need all the help they can get in keeping this company in business and growing profit-wise.

2. I know that "profits" is not a dirty word but stands for an absolute necessity. When we make reasonable profits we reward

our investors (shareholders) for their confidence in us and we gain funds to make continuous improvements, even to taking some risks of adventure into new areas.

3. I will refuse to guard my small section of the corporation, saying that whatever happens is someone else's responsibility. I feel responsible for my corporation because its total structure (not just my cubicle) gives me the protection I need.

4. I will go to my boss (or others when appropriate) with ideas and suggestions as to how we can cut down on expenses and increase profits. I do this in my own home so it is only logical that I would do it on the job as well. The more money the corporation makes, the better opportunities there are for me to share in it.

5. The best attitude I can have is one of total commitment to the purposes of the corporation. Its best purposes are providing products and services to the American public and the world, of providing jobs and security to its employees, of profits to its investors, of opportunities for all of us to prove ourselves as managers and executives.

6. Where the corporation is unresponsive, say to minority interests, to social demands, to human values, I will work to draw attention to these areas and to do all I can to help develop responsive programs to solve them.

Do *you* owe anything to your corporation? You know the answer to that question.

Checkpoint CHARLIE: what are you doing to become more effective?

This checkpoint brings you face to face with these searching questions:

1. What are *you* doing to develop the qualities of executiveship that will take you to the top?

2. What are *you* doing to make yourself more attractive to your family, friends, subordinates, neighbors, and peers?

3. What are *you* doing to build up your self-esteem, your confidence, your poise, and your emotional control?

Questions, questions, questions! Yet if you don't make the effort to answer these basic inquiries, you may very well void your efforts to improve your lot in life. Let's take them one at a time.

1. What are you doing to develop the qualities of executiveship that will take you to the top?

The qualities that are most admired by presidents and other people at the top in picking you for promotion include these:

- *Ability to make decisions* rapidly and well, on the basis of your thorough study of the situation and your previous experiences.

- *Aggressiveness* in tackling the workload, a self-starter in that you don't have to be prodded, a doer in that you follow through and complete your assignments and projects.

- *Judgment* based on your knowledge of your corporation, of its markets and competitors, of its problems and successes, of your experiences in the field of human relations.

- *Ability to motivate* the people under your management to do consistently good work, to go a bit beyond the usual self-controlled work limits to achieve greater results. In other words, leadership.

- *Enthusiasm,* a resistance to the "daily grind" and the temptation to settle down into a rut. This also means a sense of optimism that problems can be overcome and that the corporation *is* going places.

- *Adaptiveness,* staying out of the rut by being able to adjust to new people, new situations, changes in the "old order," and by turning change into advantages for yourself and the corporation.

- *Competency,* which means you know what you're talking about.

- *Loyalty,* to the people who pay your salary and who help you rise up through the ranks.

- *Ambition,* because without a strong sense of ambition you're not going to go anywhere in this world. Ambition is the sparkplug that makes you move ahead.
- *Social and community involvement,* which means that you do more than just show up for work, that you're not only aware of the problems in the city and suburbs and nation but that you're joining in the non-business groups to help solve some of them.
- *Honesty,* a word which still is not out of date. It means you can be trusted with financial responsibility, with secrets, and even with a box of paper clips.
- *Humility,* in that you don't believe the world starts and ends with you, nor that you created it and rested on the seventh day.
- *Humor,* so that you can laugh at yourself and others when ridiculous things happen and not take everything to heart as if it were a personal insult or attack.
- *Common sense,* the ability not to be impulsive and go off the deep end but look for the "why" when things go wrong. Getting to the root cause of problems calmly and objectively and solving the problems with solid, basic actions is good common sense.

These are some of the good traits that you are supposed to have. Most likely you have them all in some degree or other. Your problem is: How well does your top management *understand* that you have these qualities?

That's your task, getting credit for your good points. The only assurance that I can give you is that if you *demonstrate* these qualities day after day, top management can't help but notice them.

The qualities the people at the top do not like include these:
- *Isolation,* not being easily accessible to people
- *Abrasiveness,* the ability to get everyone about you upset
- *Dullness,* not being flexible, adaptive, curious, aggressive
- *Impatience,* getting sore at people when they don't perform as fast as you want them to
- *Lack of direction,* not knowing where you're going or what you want

- *Boorishness,* boring everyone with your sense of importance
- *Softness,* the inability to stand up for what you believe in
- *Narrow-mindedness,* seeing only what you want to see, believing only what you want to believe
- *Brittleness,* being unable to accept change, the desire to keep things forever the "way they used to be"
- *Complacency,* which allows you to feel that someone else should do the work and you'll just coast along the way you are
- *Negativisim,* having a closed mind about anything you're not sure of, a strong "It-can't-be-done" attitude. It's also an excuse for not getting busy and doing something to solve a problem. Remember the line, "You can't beat City Hall"? Pure negativism. City Hall has been beaten plenty of times by people not hampered by negative mindedness.

You can do something to make yourself more effective by assessing your qualities as honestly as you can. The good qualities you have are already well ingrained in you. Keep working on polishing them.

You'll resist looking in the mirror of your personal conduct to see what bad qualities you have. Why emphasize them? Most of us seldom want to be fully aware of our bad sides. Spend some time contemplating the various ways you act and the ways in which you handle things. If there are areas where you feel a bit sensitive, the chances are you're shielding yourself from admitting that you have a bad quality hiding there. Get to work changing those bad habits into good ones. It's no crime to have bad qualities. It's a crime to keep them for any length of time.

Now, let's take a look at how you can work harder in another important area.

2. What are you doing to make yourself more attractive to your family, friends, subordinates, neighbors, and peers?

Isn't it enough just to work hard at improving yourself on the job? Do you have to work at the same thing off the job, too?

You sure do.

That's the toughest thing for a lot of people to understand—that there is no let up anywhere during the day for a person who wants to reach the top. It is a full-time, day-long job. Your efforts to make yourself more effective in the office or the plant can't be turned off and on like a light bulb.

Simply stated, you can't live by a variety of standards. One standard for the job, another for your family, a third for your friends, and so on. If you are aspiring to be a quality person, that quality has to be reflected *in all your roles as a person*.

You are a:

- Manager
- Parent
- Spouse
- Relative
- Friend
- Neighbor
- Competitor
- Stranger
- Teacher
- Student
- Observer
- Belonger

Lump these all together, and you have quite a task of making yourself attractive to everyone with whom you come in contact. There are some guiding rules, most of which you know. It won't hurt to go over them once more.

1. *Be* as *considerate* of your family, neighbors, friends, and everyone else, as you are of the folks down at the office.

2. *Don't bring your frustrations home* and inflict them on your spouse, children, neighbors, friends, and relatives. You may be fully justified in your irritations, but no one at home admires a grouch!

3. *Become involved* with the problems your family members face, and be concerned with helping them solve those problems. If you say, "I have enough troubles at the office," and divorce yourself from the family problems because you consider them petty, you're creating difficulties for yourself. You must share yourself with your family and help them as much as you can, in line with the age-old policy of encouraging people to stand on their own two feet.

4. *Be consistent.* Some people work hard at the plant or office, then come home and loaf every evening and all weekends. Use

your energies around the house and with the family. Be active. Do your share of the housework. Participate in the activities of the children and your spouse.

5. *Demonstrate your love and acceptance.* In the field of human relations you can't take chances that all the members of your family know you love them, that you accept them individually for what they are. You must show them by your actions and by what you say (at least occasionally), so that there is no misunderstanding on these important points.

6. *Spread your enthusiasm.* You're a teacher with family credentials. Teach them enthusiasm, optimism, joy of accomplishment, the confident feeling of being their own person.

7. *Be dependable.* The feeling today that "it's none of my business" what my friends and neighbors do is very prevalent. This is another "I-won't-get-involved" cop out. Dependability as a person rests on your ability to involve yourself positively with everyone around you, not just with the folks down at the office.

3. What are you doing to build up your self-esteem, your confidence, your poise, and your emotional control?

It all comes back to you. You are the only person who can give you the kind of internal strength that you need in order to climb to the top in the business world.

When it is all said and done, *you* are the one who must build the strong type of self-esteem you need to keep going. Confidence and poise can be developed only after a long period of time and after a great deal of trial and error and of doing things properly. Emotional control is a lifelong challenge. Some days you'll do fine, other days you'll fall apart.

Emotional control is really the key to everything else. Emotional control allows you to stand on your own feet without being hopped up by drugs or alcohol. With emotional control, you gain the independence you seek and can use your abilities to master the art of managing others, of becoming an executive.

Again, let's review that familiar set of guidelines that all of us must follow in order to keep our emotions under control as much as possible:

1. I'll have beautiful days when I can do almost no wrong.
2. I'll have acceptable days when I do well but not perfectly.
3. I'll have days when I'll wish I'd stayed home, when everything seems to go wrong.
4. My emotional goal at the moment is to keep myself free of anxiety, irritations, and upsetting moods—so that I can do what is good for me and my family.
5. I will free myself from the conflicts that started with my childhood days and my parents and which I've unconsciously brought with me into adulthood.
6. I'm mature and I know I can be the master of my own life.
7. If I want to cut myself to pieces I can indulge in hatred, hostility, feelings of revenge, of being persecuted, of resenting others' successes.
8. If I want to slow down, even stop, my rise to the top, all I need to do is to act in arrogance, not give a damn about anyone else, push my weight around, live for today and forget tomorrow, and not give anyone else any consideration at all.
9. I know the mind can do funny things, particularly imagining that I've been insulted or slighted or that someone is taking advantage of me. If I think in this way I'll try to use a power play against the person I suspect, and I'll be wrong every time.
10. If I feel fatigue, I should realize right away that I'm bugging out from facing a problem squarely. I'm giving myself an out by pretending to be so tired that I can't function.
11. I know that the experts say a feeling of inferiority is a disaster for the guy or gal who owns it. If I feel inferior I'll remind myself that I've already accomplished a lot, that I've had successes, that I am confident, and that I am *not* inferior to anyone. An inferiority complex is a negative emotion, not a fact.
12. Every time I become afraid that I'll fail I start getting mad at myself. This is stupid. I know I'll fail once in a while, and it

hasn't killed me yet or resulted in my being deported from the United States. I'll expect things to go wrong at times, and I'll stop expecting to fail at things I'm trying to do.

13. My dissatisfaction is a prompter for me to go out and do things to get ahead, to change things, to learn new ways and techniques, to enter into new fields. I don't want ever to be 100 percent satisfied. Being a little dissatisfied keeps me moving in the right direction.

14. I know I learn things best when the heat is on me and the going is tough. No one learns things when life is soft. Learning comes the hard way, through struggling with adversity, through coping with problems, through putting my wits to work as often as I can every day.

15. I'll try to see myself in a positive light—as a person who has accomplished much, who has the capability to grow, mature further, and become an executive at the top. I won't allow my childish emotions to picture me in a negative light that will take the steam out of my drive toward the executive suite.

By now you must have arrived at some definite conclusions.

You can make it to the top.

You can enjoy doing it.

You can get some of the things out of life that you want.

You can win, instead of lose.

You can build your own world, because you know that your wrong emotions *can* be controlled. You know that you *can fail* once in a while without hurting yourself, that greater successes are based on your freedom from anxiety about failing at all.

The key is that you have learned to forgive yourself for your very human emotions. You have learned to know yourself as part imperfect, part perfect. You can admit that you have some goofy emotions, but can face up to them and conquer them by understanding where they come from and that they are *unreal*.

You know that we're sometimes in trouble with ourselves because we bring childhood emotions with us into our adult years. We're still trying to please our parents by "coming home with good report cards" or "doing better than Sally or Johnny did" at Little League or whatever.

Your evaluation of yourself has shown you some conclusive points about yourself. You know you have good potentials for continued success in business. You know you can continue to learn new ways and methods. You know you can continue to polish your professional and personal self.

Now you're ready to ignite yourself and move more rapidly to where you want to go. To more challenges, to more achievements, to more personal significance, to more money. To the top.

CHAPTER TEN

Why the Lessons of Today Will Make You the Leader of Tomorrow

"The trouble with 'tomorrow' is that you must get through 'today' to arrive there," a neighbor told me with a smile.

You *know* that the way you are *today* you are not fully prepared to be the executive you hope to be *tomorrow*. You have a lot of work to do in preparing yourself for the tough work that comes along with that big title. It is no secret that the lessons of today are very important in hardening you for the bigger job ahead. In this final chapter we'll take sharp looks at some of the critical areas where the lessons of today can help you in your forward progress toward the executive suite.

Ten reasons why people fail

More people fail than make it to the top. The human being is a very failure-prone critter, able to rise to amazing heights under certain circumstances but most likely to fail somewhere along the route and to gather dust and bitterness.

Why do people fail? In my many years of studying "persons on the go," the "person most likely to succeed," the "ones who've got it," and the individuals who seemed on the verge of being "real star performers," I've come to some definite conclusions. I can sum them up in "ten reasons."

Failure 1: Inability to serve the boss properly. More people end up in Nowheresville because they failed to "make it" with their boss. Insubordination, as I mentioned in an earlier chapter, just isn't tolerated for any length of time. If a manager is hot in some areas, some bosses may look the other way and temporarily ignore insubordination. But they'll never forget it, and few of them forgive it. As soon as the usefulness of such a person begins to dim, they'll find a way to get rid of the troublemaker.

Why do so many get in trouble with their bosses? The question isn't hard to answer. Bosses can be notoriously touchy about a lot of things. Being at the top makes many bosses edgy and supersensitive. They need help, they want it quick, and they want it right.

I know one manager who was given an assignment by her boss. When she got deep in the assignment, the manager discovered some new elements which confused her. Since her boss was out of town, she went to another executive and even to her boss's superior to ask advice. Her boss found out about these "advice" meetings and was furious. The manager was subsequently transferred, with the blunting of her career. Why?

She had "failed" her own boss by not telephoning him to ask instructions or waiting until the boss returned to the office to take up her questions. In her eagerness to get the job done, she'd gone to the other executive, unaware that her boss viewed *that* executive as a mortal contender for the next promotion. Dealing with the *enemy* is unforgivable in the eyes of many bosses. And going to the boss's superior was clearly a case of "going over his head," *an egregious sin.*

How about your boss? Never forget that you are there to serve your boss, not to cause her or him problems and not to do anything that can be considered "insubordination."

Failure 2: Total preoccupation with self. "I love me, why don't you love me as much?" This is what some persons seem to be saying with their actions. These individuals have a lot of drive. They are intelligent and make it quite far up the ladder because their intense infatuation with themselves gives them an extra amount of zip. Often they are extremely talented. But all that self-adoration!

They feel that every little thing they do is a "news bulletin" to everyone else. They insist on telling you everything they've done because they don't want to deprive you of the excitement of knowing the beauty of their activities. No matter what course the conversation takes, they'll find a quick way to focus it back on themselves.

You're familiar with some examples of this failure. And a failure they are. They have so little time for *other* people that they become one-dimensional to most people. They usually come on so strong that they turn us off. If they hold positions of power, they are insufferable. They never suspect that they bore the stuffing out of everyone around them. They fail because sooner or later their inability to see anything except themselves causes them to make serious mistakes in judgment, evaluation, and action. They bomb out in grand style.

I saw one such self-lover get his comeuppance. A secretary, tiring of his posturing, waited until St. Valentine's Day, when she pinned a huge valentine on the bulletin board with the executive's photo pasted in the center. It was signed by him (a forgery) *and addressed to himself.* Not a complete solution but very effective!

Failure 3: Lack of feeling for others. A kissin' cousin of self-adoration is a deep inconsideration of other people. Many a manager and many an executive is guilty of not being aware that other people are human.

Individuals who are afflicted with this character disease usually feel, "I'm too busy getting mine in this world to worry about other people." This attitude is clearly evident in what they do and say. Some of them had bad experiences with harsh individuals during their early years and settled into a "to-hell-with-them" attitude in the way they regard other people in the office and the plant.

Managers who aren't aware that other people are human are heading for trouble. If they don't know that other people can feel hurt, can feel the sharp pain of their indifference, can be frustrated by their inconsiderateness and lack of personal involvement with them, then they can't become anything like a leader of others. By cutting themselves off from them they damage their ability to move upward.

A good feeling toward others, a sensitivity to their humanness, is an essential ingredient in a top manager's makeup. It is an ingredient necessary to becoming a top executive. He or she needs to be able to feel compassion for others and their problems and struggles. He needs not to set himself apart from them but to become as much aware of them as he is of himself.

When he doesn't, he is a failure. He is a different kind of failure from the person who is totally preoccupied with himself. But he *has* failed in one of life's greatest challenges—understanding of others and sympathy for their human condition.

Failure 4: Closed door to further knowledge. Managers who have stopped learning have throttled down nearly dead in their tracks. They aren't about to make it much farther. They have stopped growing and started the process of mentally withering.

Why is it so important to learn more? A ridiculous question. There are so many things to learn, that's why! A manager on the way to becoming an executive is eternally a student.

Then why do so many managers keep their minds closed to further knowledge? Human inertia. Many people, managers or not, simply come to a point in life where it is an effort to do anything new each day. They sink into the comfort of daily routine. They love the familiar pattern which offers no changes, no bumps and jolts. They're not going anywhere except to the office each day.

How can a manager be promoted to a bigger job without demonstrating the ability to take on larger tasks and learn new methods, new techniques, new technologies, new meanings? If you were president of your company, would you promote someone who has a poor track record of reading newspapers and trade journals, attending seminars, asking questions, volunteering for work in new areas?

A closed mind to new ways is a closed door to advancement. Whenever I meet a person who brags about never reading a newspaper or a business publication, I know I've met a closed door.

Failure 5: Inability to be persuasive of own good ideas. Years ago I used to sit in a staff meeting every morning in which we discussed the day's work programs and contributed our ideas and suggestions.

Often I knew more about a subject than anyone else in the room, but whenever I opened my mouth to speak someone else had the floor. Many of the meetings would end without my getting my ideas across.

When I at last became painfully aware of how inadequate I was, I got busy and learned to be more articulate. I took night courses in psychology, and I joined a self-help speaking group, Toastmasters International. That, plus my desire, enabled me to break the ice, and since then I seldom have been troubled in being persuasive about my own good ideas. But it took strong effort on my part.

Being persuasive is never easy. Some individuals are fluent talkers. Some never seem to shut up. Most, however, are reserved in meetings and speak only when they feel they must. The person who sits in a meeting, hiding behind a pipe, cigar, cigarette, or frown or appearance of deep concentration, actually is copping out.

The person who is afraid to go in and sit down with the boss and present new ideas is defeating the management system which could work in his or her behalf. The boss wants ideas—good, solid, well-thought-out ideas. If you're convinced your ideas are worthwhile, *speak up.* You can put them into a memo form if no regular meeting is immediately available.

The fear of rejection or of looking silly keeps many individuals from volunteering their own good ideas and of being persuasive about their effectiveness. It is a human fear, unfortunately, and it leads to failure for the man or woman who does have good ideas but can't find the courage to get them across to others.

Failure 6: Unawareness of the realities of the business world. Are you a dingaling? A meathead? There are plenty of Archie Bunker types in the business world. They see only what they want to see. Their ideas of how a company functions are limited to whatever types of narrow mind they possess.

The business world is unavoidably becoming more complex each year. The executive-in-training has to cope with a great many realities. There are problems in labor-management, raw materials acquisition, production, distribution, marketing, pricing, on and on. All these are under constant change—perhaps precipitously, perhaps slowly, but always a change.

When men and women enter the business world the newness of it makes a tremendous impression on them. Unfortunately, that impression remains for a very long period of time with people who are basically inflexible. "This is not the way we did it years ago," they'll say. Or, "It was better around here when I started." They can't adjust to the realities; they prefer to keep their illusions.

The realities of the business world require that enterprising managers see for themselves how some markets are drying up, how others are emerging, how the national character is undergoing change, how the industry they are in is being altered by competition (domestically and internationally), and how situations that were once a solid rock are now eroded into piles of sand.

Top management changes, too, and this has a tremendous impact on the reality of a business. The new people coming in always change things. It is a reality of life. "It was nicer around here under the old president," a manager could say. A touching tribute but not squaring with the reality of life in the business world.

Failure 7: Lack of creative imagination. What *is creative imagination?* It's the kind of imagination that allows a manager to develop creative actions of leadership.

"I've met a great many managers who are totally devoid of imagination," a top advertising executive related at lunch one day. "They learn a routine, and that's it. No tinkering with it, no experimentation, no trying it a different way, no challenging of set methods. To them it is almost akin to rape, burglary, or robbery to suggest challenging the system."

Yet it is *new ideas* which lead to improved methods. It is *creative thinking* which examines current practices and finds ways for things to be done faster and better and at less cost. It is *imagination* which allows the mind to leap past barriers and see the new horizons of the future.

Business today needs all the creative imagination it can get. Tremendous improvements have already been scored by men and women who have not been trapped by dull routine. They were able to use their imagination and come up with ideas and plans for great improvement in products, merchandising, customer relations, technologies, what have you.

A manager who does not *try* to use creative imagination may become rooted firmly to one spot in a corporation. There this individual may be entirely dependable in routine drudgery. But for a more challenging job, where a free and eager mind is necessary, the same person may be entirely out of place.

Failure 8: The wrong chemistry of character. I've heard it many times. "The *chemistry* between them wasn't right," or, "She was the *wrong* person for that job," or "He lacked the *character* to handle the job."

These were individuals who had gained a good executive job and had failed. What went wrong? *Character.*

Character is difficult to describe. It's a sort of hidden control panel inside you. I've heard it said that character is what you are when no one else is around. It is, to others, a method of identifying you. "He's a *real* character!" means you do some outlandish things. "She has *no* character" means that you are undependable, create suspicion about yourself, are guilty of pulling off shady things, do backstabbing, double-deal others, and are outrageously competitive.

A person's character is inescapable. Think of the type of character that Washington, Jefferson, Monroe, Lincoln, Eisenhower, and other great American presidents had. Think of the type of character some of our great writers had. Think of the questionable character some of our movie greats and our celebrated politicians have had.

Good managers, trying to elevate themselves to the executive suite, can't make it unless they understand that they are judged to some extent *on the type of character they represent*. Character to the people at the top means a hidden control panel that governs you in such a way that you can be trusted, that you try to see both sides of any question, that you sincerely want to help the corporation stay in business and prosper . . . that you're not just out for yourself.

Failure 9: The personality cult. Closely allied with the failures who lacked feeling for other people and were totally preoccupied with themselves are the highly competitive managers or executives who try to create their own personality cult. The massive ego of some men and women compels them to surround themselves with business lackeys who are subservient to them and who feed their ravenous appetite for approval. They are usually in competition with someone for a bigger title. One of the biggest guns they shoot off is, "Look at me, I'm in charge of all these people! That means I *must* be the better person!"

Women and men on ego trips often are extremely talented. But they are driven, driven by a terrifying anxiety that they *are not* admired and envied. They are compelled to strive for the very top to try to vanquish their unconscious fear that they are inadequate, ineffective, unwanted, unappreciated. The *cover* for their motivations is that *they* are better qualified to have that top job because they have more people reporting to them than someone else has.

Men and women on ego trips are everywhere in the business world. They are not unusual at all. They give themselves away because of their insistence that anyone who works with them pay them some sort of regular homage. In a way, it's a throwback to the royalty of old who insisted that their subjects publicly "pledge" themselves to them.

The personality cult often fails because the business lackeys who make up the cult have a habit of jumping ship, deserting, transferring. Only the strongest, most magnetic ego can keep the sycophants clustered around it for any length of time. Even so, the structure often is doomed to fall of its own motionless weight.

Failure 10: The gamblers. These are the men and women who have a compulsion to take ridiculous chances in the business world. Not with *their* money, naturally. With the *corporation's*. Despite all the solid indicators against it, they want to "try something different." The underlying motivation is that they are convinced they have a special knack of divining the outcome of a business adventure.

They are the ones who plug hard for a new product, even though there may be no market for that product. Or their company can't make it cheap enough to satisfy the market. Or it would come out after the competitors have picked the market clean.

Why do men and women of this type want to take such chances? For a simple reason. They feel they can pull off a "big one," win acclaim and approval, and show that they're a real leader. If it worked out the way they're convinced it would, they could do all that. But the graveyard of the business world is littered with the bones of managers and executives who felt they possessed some great knack of knowing what will happen.

Some corporations do take calculated gambles. Some win, some lose. Most corporations want to make their moves after they have painfully studied the situation and carefully lined up their ducks all in a row. If they are beckoned down the garden path by a manager or executive who proves to be a gambler and not a leader, they'll gladly ship that individual's bones to the business world's graveyard.

Only a gambler who wins is loved. Never one who loses.

Ten reasons why men and women succeed

Out of hundreds, we've just reviewed ten reasons why some men and women fail. Would you like to take a look at *ten reasons why many men and women succeed?*

In the great area of human endeavor "doing the opposite" of what the failures did isn't enough. It isn't "not doing bad things." It is mainly doing positive things that pushes a manager upward and enhances him as a budding executive.

Of the hundreds of positive things that people do to help themselves succeed, I've chosen ten from the suggestions of the executives I've interviewed that I feel are the most representative.

Success 1: The balanced person. In contrast to the "workaholic," the person who devotes every waking minute to the job, is the balanced person. The only thing remarkable about a balance person is the tremendous difficulty in becoming one. The balanced person feels this way:

The job is important and while I'm at work I'll do the very best I can.

But there is more to life than a job and a corporation . . . there are family, friends, neighbors, the community, social groups, and the like. They all will get their fair share of attention, too.

I'll enjoy weekends, vacations, holidays without bringing home a briefcase jammed with work. I'll relax when I can, read a good book, take the family on a picnic or to a movie. *I'll live a little as well as work a lot.*

Success 2: The uncrushables. Uncrushable people are smart enough to set reasonably attainable goals for themselves. In this way, they won't crush themselves in a fall if they try to climb too high too fast and lose their grip.

Disaster strikes many individuals whose hopes and aspirations far outdistance their abilities to get what they want out of life. The uncrushables have seen disaster strike other people. They know that all of us have limitations. They know they can reach pretty high in life if they pace themselves, prepare themselves, remain flexible, and stay in there plugging. They know they'll have some reverses, that they won't win everything they set their hearts on.

But they remain uncrushed because they understand the complexities and realities of the business world. If they have lost something yesterday, they'll refuse to take it as a personal rejection. They'll continue to work for something they might gain tomorrow.

Too many men and women stop in their tracks when they are crushed by an event in the business world. They turn bitter and resentful. The uncrushables take the hammering in stride and go on. They'll go as high as they can, and they accept what they get, not what they fantasize about.

Success 3: The sense-of-humor person. I can think of scores of men and women in business who would have "gone out of their skulls" with the pressure if they hadn't possessed a good sense of humor. You might even be one of them!

The ability to see the funny side of a serious situation can keep an individual loose, flexible, and capable of snapping back. Not that every serious situation can be viewed from a "funny side." Often there is just a somber, semitragic side about things that go wrong. But it is equally semitragic if people drag themselves around with long faces and funereal tones. When something goes deathly wrong it should be analyzed, a lesson should be learned, and the persons involved should be off on corrective actions.

Humor has a very smoothing effect, and the individual who can insert a bit of humor into a serious situation can contribute a great deal to the group's ability to bounce back and get things going again.

Life is too short for long periods of mourning for business tragedies. No one has ever said that everything *must* go right every time. There are going to be plenty of crises each year. Life doesn't stop. It goes on, and it goes on better when a manager has a sense of humor and sees the light side, as well as a sense of responsibility and sees the serious side.

Success 4: The involved person. The tendency today in the

business world is for a person to go inward instead of outward toward other people. It's a lousy tendency.

The involved person resists this pull, knows that going inward is going nowhere and knows that the real fun of life is in being involved in a number of selected activities. He starts his involvement in activities that help his corporation, such as joining association, civic, environmental, and industrial groups, and the like.

He continues his involvement where it will help his family, in local, educational, governmental, religious, political, and fraternal groups. He takes sides in political situations and goes to the polls to vote. If he has a decided opinion he'll attend town hall meetings and make himself heard. He may even write an occasional letter to the editor and get his views across to hundreds and thousands of other people.

He likes to invite friends over for dinner, and instead of relying solely on booze or television to carry the evening he serves up an interesting conversation on local, national, and international subjects.

He cooperates in the recycle efforts to save paper, glass, and aluminum. He cooperates in keeping his part of the neighborhood clean and attractive. He doesn't litter, and he doesn't waste. He doesn't ignore bad situations. He reports them to the proper authorities.

The involved person is a good spouse, a good parent, a fine neighbor, and an excellent citizen.

The involved person makes the best kind of manager and executive.

Success 5: The learner. The learner and the involved individual are often (but not necessarily) the same person.

The learner has come to the conclusion that he or she does *not* know everything worth knowing. This is a refreshing admission. Too many people seem to think they've cornered the market on knowledge. Not the learners.

They read the business press, the daily newspaper; they take books out of the public library, even buy books at their local bookstore. They attend trade association meetings to pick up tips on how they can do their job better or how the corporation can save time, money, and effort. They're curious and ask many questions. They'll volunteer for assignments at the office in order to learn more methods.

The more they learn the better managers they become. And the better managers they become, the more they assure themselves of making it up into the executive ranks. They make their efforts to gain more knowledge pay off.

Success 6: The failure killer. All people fear failure. They fear looking bad in other people's eyes. They fear being blamed if things go wrong. They fear looking silly, or stupid, or dumb, or incompetent. They try to play everything as safe as they can and to look as good as they can in everyone's eyes.

This sort of thing makes a nervous wreck out of millions of people. Not so with the failure killer.

The failure killers know two important facts of life. Fact one—you can't win them all. Fact two—*you can't lose them all.* If they lose one, they don't feel pity for themselves. He plays the percentages. He knows the more activities he manages the more he'll win. He refuses to let a few failures dim the luster of the times when he wins.

Success 7: The sensitive person. Sensitive toward *others,* that is.

The ego of most men and women, particularly those with strong drives toward success, often diverts them from thinking much about other people. Business persons can be boorish toward cab drivers, elevator operators, store clerks, long-distance telephone operators, their own secretaries and underlings. They can be unthinking about their own spouses, sons, daughters, neighbors, friends, colleagues, and acquaintances.

The sensitive person has done some thinking on the subject and is aware of how business look to others. He's aware that it takes very little effort to be courteous and considerate of other people, especially those less fortunate than he is.

He'll contribute to charitable fund drives. He'll smile at people who wait on him and say, "Thank you." He'll refuse to get crusty at a confused or busy store clerk. He'll treat women with equality, be polite without overdoing it.

He keeps his own ego intact but not at the expense of mistreating or taking advantage of other people.

Success 8: The respectful person. Respectful persons respect themselves. They found a way to overcome self-doubts and deep anxiety. They learned that we all have a certain amount of self-hatred in us. They discovered that as long as they held on to their self dislike they were getting nowhere. They began to see that if they could find things about themselves of which they honestly were proud, things of substance (not purely of ego), that enabled them to both live with themselves more comfortably and accomplish more at work.

They began to look for the positive approaches to themselves. If they blundered or goofed, they felt bad for a short time and went on to other things. They worked hardest in those areas where they knew they felt more at home and could score more achievements.

As more achievements came along, their self-respect grew. They came to understand that every man or woman is a mixture of blunders and successes, that it is best to concentrate on the things that breed self-respect than on things that breed self-hate.

Some people never learn this lesson. They spend all of their lives learning not to like themselves. And it's such a waste of energy, energy that could have been used creating the positive building blocks of a successful and contented life.

Success 9: The forgiving person. It's easy to dislike other people. It's easy to find things about them that irritate you or turn you off. Just look and you'll find them. See what crazy things people do and it's no problem to scorn them and build up a good hate for them. All the more so if they're older or younger, are of another skin color, race, or religion, or come from a different part of the country or from a different social stratum.

A forgiving person came through the darkness of dislike, distrust, and disassociation. She found that particular darkness was like a circular path in the heavy forest. It got her nowhere. When she began to forgive people for appearing different, or thinking differently, or acting differently, she began to feel free.

She had men and women who acted selfishly against her, people who stretched the truth, people who baited her or took advantage of her. Instead of hating them, she found that she could forgive them. It made it tremendously more easy for her to go on to other things that would benefit her. She came to the conclusion that some people would treat her badly, but that most people would treat her with consideration. Her freedom from nagging hate enabled her to spend her energies getting somewhere.

Success 10: The corporation person. The average American pictures the corporation person as a slave, some kind of relentless nut who is a workaholic, neglects his family, spends every night at the office or in traveling, and burns himself out in his forties, never having known what it is like to be a family man or to take a relaxing vacation, who is unknown by his sons and daughters, and who is interested only in the almighty dollar and the almighty big title on the door.

I've met some of these individuals, but not many. The real corporation persons are not antagonistic to the company that pays their salary, nor are they a slave to it. They don't neglect their family, their friends, or themselves to put in a massive amount of free time working for the corporation.

Instead they have solid respect for the organization, for its history of accomplishments, for the many other fine men and women who work for it. They don't accuse it of being the enemy of "the public," of being almost sinister in its methods of "making profits for the shareholders." They see the mistakes it makes, and understand how they were made. They see the positive accomplishments, and they know how hard the people in the corporation worked to score those successes.

Corporation people are a blend of the other nine successes. They don't overkill things with too much emotion. They don't ignore things, don't have a smug lack of interest. They know that all business organizations are imperfect, held together loosely by the people who manage them, capable of monstrous mistakes, yet also capable of fantastic achievements. Corporation people use all their control functions to work within the corporation to help it achieve more of its goals and to overcome more of its weaknesses.

They take their paycheck, and they do not bite the hand that gives it to them. They are balanced, learners, failure killers, uncrushable, of good humor, involved, sensitive, respectful, and forgiving. They're great gals and guys, and they're on the way to the top.

Ten reasons why YOU can make it

We've really been talking about *you*, haven't we? In this chapter you've seen yourself quite a bit. You've spotted some of the "good you" and some of the "bad you." You know that no matter what your age or where you are on the ladder of success, there is still much work you must do in equipping yourself for the job at the top that you want.

You can make it.

The top has always been there. It is available to you if you can develop yourself further into the type of person who deserves to win a place at the top.

You can make it for a number of good reasons. The reasons below are based on your *attitude,* not on "good fortune," not on "luck," not on "knowing somebody big," and not on "getting the breaks." *They are based on your ability not to defeat yourself.* Let's take a look at them.

Reason 1. You can handle your responsibility in holding costs to an acceptable minimum. Your sense of responsibility is large enough that it motivates you to get your work done on schedule. It makes you work for the good of the corporation as much as you work for your own betterment, to try to help profits no matter what the business conditions may be.

Reason 2. You are not contemptuous of your job, your corporation, your business associates, or your life-style. You don't berate yourself because at this point in your life you haven't made it as high as you wanted. You don't feel you made such a bad choice in going to work for your corporation. You don't look at your associates as if they are the dregs of humanity. You don't complain because your income and status restrict you to your present life-style. You *know* that it is up to you to improve any of these conditions. You're determined to do just that.

Reason 3. You have escaped the deadly lethargy that sets in when a person feels that the way upward is blocked by uncontrollable forces. You *know* that you do control your own destiny. You *know* that individuals are blocked only to the extent that they *allow* themselves to be impeded by circumstances or other people.

Reason 4. You can avoid that "sense of helplessness" that comes to some people when they are faced with the massive problems of working with unions, of getting production snarls ironed out, of meeting the threats of skilled competition, of meeting arbitrarily imposed deadlines, of acquiring a greatly extended knowledge to deal with new things, new methods, new technologies, new people. You break all these challenges down into easily handled fragments that you can manage.

Reason 5. You fight those seemingly uncontrollable urges to eat too much, enjoy cocktails too much, enjoy night life too much, pamper yourself too much. There are nearly uncontrollable urges to be mean, to fight back, to make cutting remarks, to put people in their places, to rebel against what seems to be impossible conditions. You *know* these urges can easily become actions if unleashed by a person's poor emotional control. You *know* that control is absolutely essential to your progress, that uncontrollable urges will make it extremely difficult for you to get from life the things you desire.

Reason 6. You refuse to be taken in by one of humankind's greatest emotional con artists—the feeling that you've "been had." This emotion is a poison that has felled many promising managers. They conclude, for whatever reasons, that the corporation or a group of executives has "taken them in and done them dirt." No one, my friend, ever has "been had." The situation exists only in the minds of individuals who are superanxious, supersensitive, who didn't perform the way they should have, and who let the competition walk away from them. They defaulted. Their ego defense: They've "been had." Not you. You *know* better. You *know* you lose only when you allow yourself to lose.

Reason 7. You are turned on, not turned off. A deeply dissatisfied manager often will feel, "I won't do much to help my boss because he isn't doing much to help me." That manager feels the work is boring, not meaningful, that he or she is getting nowhere because the boss won't pep up the job and make it exciting and interesting. The blame falls on the boss, so the idea is, "The hell with him." You avoid this emotional trap. You *know* you have a choice, to be turned on or to be turned off. You turn yourself on to get ahead and go places.

Reason 8: You are aware of the tragedy of an "obsession with winning." The total emphasis on winning every little victory degrades you. It debases human endeavor. An individual simply can't win all the time, because no one is perfect and no situation lends itself to absolute victory. You *know* you'll get your ears pinned back occasionally. You *know* you'll do some dumb things. You *know* you'll get caught leaning off first base—once in a while. You'll settle for being a normal human being, shrug off your defeats, and go on to win as much as you can.

Reason 9: You are a realist, changing yourself to meet the demands of your world. You decide not to make the ridiculous mistake many other people make, of trying to change the world to suit their needs. There is no one more bitter than the person who comes to understand that all the ranting and shouting at the world hasn't changed it one bit. Politicians fit this mold; so do radicals, far-out liberals, bleeding-heart novelists, underground pamphleteers. The most effective changes any individual makes start with those he makes in his or her attitudes, actions, outlook, expectations, emotions. Realists live longer, achieve more, and are much more at home in this sometimes idiotic world of ours.

Reason 10: You relate to others. You fully understand how important other people are to you, to help you in your lifetime struggle to live within your human shell. You know that "living for yourself" isn't satisfying in the long term to a normal person. You know that the deep richness of life comes from a warm involvement with your family and friends. You find delightful rewards in sharing your successes with those whom you love and who love you. You find reassurance in their affection when things occasionally go a bit rough in your human course. You'll hear some people say that "everyone is out for himself," and you'll refuse to apply this to *everyone*. The vast majority of Americans are wonderful people, capable of deep warmth for others, eager to help when they're needed, proud of their heritage, hard workers at their jobs, solid, dependable citizens, in every sense of the term. Relating open-heartedly to others is the key not only to your success as a manager rising to executiveship but to your growth as a person.

What to do tomorrow, next month, next year, in moving upward

Your sights are set. If you suffered from tumbling thoughts, they're now straightened out. You know you want to get ahead. You have a clearer idea of where you want to go.

You see the big picture. The world does not revolve around you. You are *part* of the world, and you'll succeed to the extent that you *try* to succeed. Success is there for you to win if you equip yourself with the skills to win it. No one is keeping you from winning what you want—except you. Control yourself, and you control your movement upward toward the top.

You maintain your timetable. No one wins anything worthwhile without a game plan, a timetable. You must move consistently upward through a series of managerial chairs. You set yourself a realistic (not wishful-thinking) timetable, and you stick with it. You refuse to allow yourself to be shunted off to some back office by your own default. If you're not making the progress you feel you should, you sit down with your boss for a frank discussion of whether it is the fault of the corporation or your fault. Find out why, and do something either way to correct the situation.

You "step outside yourself." We're all lonely people "inside" ourselves. We gain strength and vitality in our ability to step outside ourselves and enjoy being with other people—at the office, at the plant, in the neighborhood, in our own family. We're like rechargeable batteries, brought up again and again to the peak of our power by refreshing contracts with those whom we love, admire, and respect.

You treat yourself humanly. Human beings have a fantastic ability to cut themselves to ribbons emotionally. None of us is all that sure that we're worthy of good things, of success, of victories. We suffer deep and painful misgivings, fears, anxieties. Giving in to these disabling emotions is giving in to failure. You will treat yourself in a human fashion, aware of your weaknesses but also aware of your strengths.

What you do tomorrow. For every tomorrow that there is you awake to the thought that *it will be a good day*. You know you'll win some, lose some, but that in the balance you will make progress. Tomorrow is always a great time to start anew. Tomorrow is always a day of a fresh start, a time to try new things, a time to adjust better, a time to work, and a time to enjoy.

What you do next month. You can measure progress more

when you compare month to month, not day to day. Looking back, you can see that you *did* achieve successes last month. You look ahead to the next month as a time to try to score even more in being a better manager, in learning more about how to be a productive executive.

What you do next year. Next year is when some promotions may be available, when pay raises might be due, when more challenges will come along to be tackled. You prepare yourself for next year by doing the very best job you can each day of this year.

How's your view of the top now?

Few people can accurately visualize how the top will be when they finally get there. They have some illusions, and these are blasted when they finally arrive where they want to be. The top is *never* what you think it's going to be. It is a shifting, changing, often gaseous state of affairs. It is never a soft, easy chair to sink into after you've won the race. Instead, it is another track meet with higher hurdles, longer broadjumps, higher pole vaults.

Looking back at a long career, a silver-haired retired executive summed it up this way. "When you arrive at the top you'll bring with you the freshness of your thinking, the strength of your personal vitality, the force of your convictions. You'll find that the top is always a mixture of new ideas and old tried-and-true ways. Every day sees a struggle to match old ideas with new ways and new ideas with old ways. Old ideas and old ways often cancel each other out. New ideas and new ways often clash explosively. At the top there is an eternal seeking of the right combinations to solve both long-standing and freshly developing problems."

He should know. His former company did more than $300 million in sales. He had brought it to that point from a $40-million-a-year enterprise.

The top is not a place to sit. The top is a place of combat, a place of seemingly quiet activity, yet electrified with an intensity and spreading into an immensity you'll never understand until, at long last, *you are part of it*.

Only when you are at the top will you clearly understand how necessary it was for you to prepare yourself solidly to withstand its pressures. Only then will you see how your weaknesses can destroy you and how your strengths can preserve you.

As it is with all things in life, you understand the top only when you are there. No one now there can adequately tell you about it as it will apply to you. The top as it exists today, with you looking up at it, will not be there when you arrive at its level. Somehow, delicately, undetectedly, without seeming to, it will have changed merely by your arrival.

In the greatest sense it has changed because *you* are the change that has entered into its hallowed suite. It will be as if you had the top with you all the time.

The "magic thoughts" that keep you refreshed.

You know that there are no "magic thoughts" to help you on your way to the top. There *are* thoughts that have the magic power of keeping your emotions on the positive track and not on the negative track. *There* is where the magic lies.

Try these:

1. I will not defeat myself by giving in easily to my wrong emotions. I'll fight for my "emotional rights."

2. I'm human and I'm making mistakes like anyone else. I'll write these mistakes down each day the best way I can, analyze them, try to understand why I'm making them. The next day I'll try to avoid making them again in a silly repeat pattern. I'll see from this record of mistakes what I'm doing wrong and work to correct them.

3. I need all the help I can get, and this means surrounding myself with friends who encourage me by setting good examples

that I can follow. I'll read books, attend lectures, visit people who inspire me, do everything I can in order to stimulate myself and keep refreshed my desire to succeed.

4. When I do things right, I'll congratulate myself with the knowledge that I'm managing to bring things together rather well. When I do things wrong, I'll not shrug it off but look inside myself to find out what it is that I'm doing wrong. In a way, I'm still like a little kid who needs to be praised or chastised. I'll never outgrow the need for this daily self-examination and need for continual improvement.

5. I won't hurt anyone else. I end up hurting myself more than I hurt them.

6. I won't think I'm some sort of golden boy or golden girl who has a magic touch. The golden ones usually turn out to be mortals who have gilded themselves, like lilies.

7. I'll look for the good side of everyone I meet. I know they have a bad side, but I'm not going to see only the bad. The good in each person is what helps me, not the bad.

8. I know I'm in a race with time. By their nature, all mortals feel they are eternal. I know better. I'm growing older each day, and there never is all the time left I would like to have. I will hurry to improve myself because without improvement I'll go nowhere in the business world, or in my personal life.

9. I live in a great nation. Despite its internal and international difficulties, it still offers me great opportunities to advance myself as an individual. I'll do all I can to help increase my country's strength and not contribute to its problems. I'll be a responsible citizen, making myself heard when I'm earnestly convinced I can make a constructive suggestion or criticism.

10. With all there is to do in trying to reach the top, I won't forget that having fun is just as important. Relaxing on a weekend, seeing the sights, going out, taking a great vaction—all this is mine to enjoy, mine to have with my family and friends. Being a workaholic is fine for short spurts but not as a complete life-style.

Go ahead, press the ignition button!

No one is holding you back. *No one* is standing before you holding up a hand to prevent you from moving upward to the executive suite. Nothing stands between you and what you want out of the business world except your *own imagination*.

Why should you deprive yourself *and your family* of the wonderful benefits your greater success in business can assure you?

Why should you labor in a lowly spot when you can lift yourself to be on the highest level of personal attainment, where the rewards are far richer?

Why should you cheat yourself of the satisfactions and sense of achievement that come from winning an executive title that *you deserve* because of your hard work and careful planning?

There was nothing new in this book. The facts in it are known to nearly every successful man and woman. If you learned one new gutsy fact in these chapters you learned that *people make themselves successes,* success does not come looking for them. Big salaries are seldom handed to people on their way up; they have to fight hard and work ceaselessly for them.

What are you waiting for? Go ahead, press the ignition button!

Burst loose from the gantry of bad emotions that hold you earthbound. Use the exotic fuel of your good emotions to propel you upward to a place at the top where you belong. Use the guidance system of your great personal initiative to win the deep sense of fulfillment that it can achieve for you.

You *have* skills and talents and capabilities. All you have to do is *ignite them* by pressing the button of your forces of personal growth.

Press the button!

Index

A

Accountability, manager of, 157
Aggression:
  collecting, 111
  as a valuable emotion, 105
Aggression level, 48–50
American Indians, 100
Anxiety, handling, 41, 73, 103
Attitudes:
  balanced, 206
  "because-it's-me," 31–32
  controlling destiny, 179–180
  corporation person, 211
  dissatisfaction, 55–57
  failure killer, 209
  forgiving, 210–211
  ground rules for, 2–7
  humor, sense of, 210
  involvement, 207–208
  learning, 208–209
  master plan, 77–78, 96–98
  mile vision, 158–161, 165
  negative, 32–34
  positive, 34–37, 52–54, 78–80

Attitudes *(Cont.):*
  respectful, 210
  sensitive, 209–210.
  tyranny, 12
  uncrushable, 206–207
Authority:
  delegation of, 155–157
  manager of, 155–157
  sharing, 112
Authority figure, resentment of, 102
Autonomy, 105–106

B

Boss:
  attention from, 80
  evaluation from, 182
  failure to serve, 198
  learning from, 89–90, 139, 185–186
  qualities of, 184–185
  reporting to, 143, 157

221

Boss *(Cont.):*
 serving, 182–183
 understanding your, 182–186
 yardstick for measuring, 69–71
Business practices:
 basic elements, 80
 challenges, 93

C

Carson, Johnny, 102
Change(s):
 areas of, 66–67
 resistance to, 73–74, 130–131
 taking place in United States business, 66–67
 as a way of humanity, 4
 welcoming, 3
Climate:
 of communications, 23
 personal, establishing, 22
Committees, controlling, 134–135
Common sense, emotional, 93–94
Communications:
 climate of, 23
 effective, 83, 85
 feedback, 86
 inward and outward, 124–126
 manager of, 154–155
Comparison, 107
Competition:
 economic, 62
 studying, 142
Competitiveness:
 avoiding, 3
 coping with competitive peers, 167–169
 neurosis of, 12
 spirit of, 131
Concepts:
 corporation, 63–64
  (*See also* Corporation)
 of executives, 67–69
Conduct, daily rules for, 90–93

Confidence, developing, 10, 74
Conflict:
 preventing, 114–116
 as a stumbling block, 99–101
 tragic side of, 116–118
 unavoidable, 14–17
 understanding, 73
Corporation(s):
 function of the, 63–66
 helping your, 186–188
 problems in a large, 94–96
 types of, 64–66
Council of Profit Sharing Industries, 85
Crisis, turning a, into a plus, 75

D

Decisions:
 avoiding, 10
 firing misfits, 136–138
 goal-setting, 180–181
 making, 60
Delegation:
 of authority, 155–157
 to overcome weaknesses, 23
 of responsibility, 148
Depression, 104, 117
Destiny, controlling, 179–180, 195–196
Discipline, self-, 63, 96
Dissatisfaction:
 as a promopter, 195
 understanding, 55–57
Domination, 106

E

Ego, 106
Emergency procedures, setting, 85
Emotional response, uplifting, 3
Emotions:
 aggression, 105

Emotions *(Cont.):*
  anxiety, 39–40
  checklist, 41–44, 178–179
  common sense, 93–94
  controlling, 9, 35–36, 72–75, 194–196
  cutting, 22
  deep-seated, 17
  disruptive, 19
  full range of, 7
  "hang fire," 102–104
  hidden, 8, 48, 101
  mature, yardstick for measuring, 87–89
  neurosis, competitive, 12
  "puppet strings," 44–45
  self-defeating, 101–102
  tension, 38
Enterprise, emphasizing, 131–132
Enthusiasm, 6
Environment, childhood, 8
Executive(s):
  appraisal of, 89–90
  becoming an, 71–72
  contributions of, 61–62
  in-training, 2
  judging you, 80–81
  measurement yardstick for, 69–71
  qualities of, 189–190
  requirements of, 62–63
  selecting goals, 67–69
  shortage of, 175–176
  types of, 58–59
  vanity of, 70

F

Failure:
  caused by lack of: character, 203–204
    creative imagination, 203
    feeling, 199–200
    learning, 200–201
  fear of, 72

Failure *(Cont.):*
  of gamblers, 205
  nonpersuasiveness, 201–202
  personality cult, 204–205
  preoccupation with self, 199
  to serve boss properly, 198
    (See also Boss)
  unawareness of realities, 202
Failures, human, firing, 136–137
Family, 46–47, 191–192
Fantasies:
  childhood, 28, 29
  promotion, 13, 117
  about what one is owed, 3
Firing, no alternatives to, 136–137
  (See also Failure)
Flexibility, attaining, 38
Forecasting, 150–151
Friends, 18, 191–192
Frustration, 72
  self-inflicted, 57

G

German concentration camps, 100
Goal:
  definition of, 180–181
  setting of, 124–127
Guilt, sense of, 103

H

Harmony, working in, 61
Hate, measures of, 8
Hostility:
  hidden, 2, 11
  unnecessary, 73
Human nature:
  complications in, 23
  peculiarities in, 22
Hurdles, management, 161–165
  (See also Management)

I

Illusions, business world, 18–19
Image, deceptive, 3
Incentives, multiple, 24, 92
Inferiority, unnecessary feeling of, 74
Innovative plan, criticizing, 31
Inquisition, the, 100
Irritation, 25

L

Leadership:
  accountability, 157
  affinity for, 50–51
  communications, 154–155
  delegating authority, 155–157
  enthusiasm, selling, 141–144
  example, setting, 127
  financial, 149–150
  forecasting, 150–151
  goal setting, 126–127
  making committees work, 134–135
  marketing, 145–146
  at meetings, 152–154
  productivity, 84–87
  profits, 148–149
  purchasing, 144–145
  qualities of, 59–61
  recruitment, 151–152
  time management, 146–147
Learning:
  leadership, 197
  lifetime task, 6
  management techniques, 6
    (*See also* Attitudes)
  about self, 35–36
  self-improvement, 71–72
Life-style, winning, 20
Listening to subordinates, 23, 125, 127–128
Love, measures of, 8

M

Management:
  aggressiveness, 48–50
  emotions, checklist of, 41–44
  good side of, 165–167
  hurdles, 161–165
  perspective in, 38, 50, 52–53
  yardstick for measuring personnel, 25–26
Managers:
  obstacle hurdling by, 49
  profit-minded, 149–150
  requirements of, 25–26
Marketing manager, 145–146
Master plan, development of, 77–78
Maturity, yardstick for measuring, 87–89
Meetings:
  displays at, 153
  improvement of, 152–153
  leadership at, 152–154
  participants at, 125
  purpose of, 152
Misfits, 172–173
Mistakes, helpful, 128–129

N

National Association of Manufacturers, 85
Needs for Improvement, 71–72
Neuroticism, 104

O

Olivier, Sir Laurence, 102
Opportunities, seeing, 62, 175–176
Organized, being, 81–82, 147

P

People:
  compromise by, 35
  escaping from, 22
  frailties of, 7
People-orientation, 61
Perfectionism as form of anxiety, 73, 103–104
Personality storms, 2
Pessimism, 6
Philosophical about winning and losing, 5
Planning:
  attitudes essential to, 34
  necessity of, 53, 76
Potentials, not using full, 101–102
Power:
  complicated, 21
  go-ahead, 78–80
  of insight, 23
  struggle for, 19–20, 70
Pressure, 71, 73
Problem solving in work flow, 83–84
Problems:
  awareness of, 16
  childhood, 28
  emotional, deep-seated, 17
  people-caused, 1
  in young adulthood, 24–30
Procrastination, 108
Productivity techniques, 84–87
Profit:
  action and, 83
  definition of, 64, 149–150
  as goal of business, 62, 80
  manager of, 148–149
Profit centers, 122
Progress, 5
  evaluating, 177
Projection, 107
Psychology:
  not defeating yourself, 212–215

Psychology *(Cont.):*
  knowing yourself, 27–30
  magic thoughts, 218–219
  measuring emotional impact of others, 1–26
  sensing what is in peoples' minds, 118–120
  stereotypes, 169–171
  upward force techniques, 20–25
Purchasing agent, 144

Q

Quinn, Anthony, 102

R

Reality, 3
Recognition:
  executive, 68
  forms, 97
  need for, 11
  spotlight, 22
Recruitment, 151–152
Regression, 108
Reporting to subordinates, 125
Responsibility:
  coping with, 52
  deep sense of, 17
  setting example, 127
Russian slave-labor camps, 100

S

Self-discipline, 63, 96
Self-esteem, 106, 117, 159–160, 176
  building, through self-help, 193–196
Self-hate, 107

Self-help:
  assessing your qualities, 188–191
  being organized, 81–82
  believing in self, 32–35, 78
  building self-esteem, 193–196
  daily conduct, 90–93
  developing attractiveness, 191–193
  gaining attention, 80–81
  meeting new people, 171–172
  new skills, 139–141
  preparing yourself for the top, 215–217
  public speaking, 174–175
Self-punishment, avoiding, 79
Selling yourself, 141–144
Skills:
  executive, polishing, 139–141
  at job levels, 6
Subordinates:
  abilities of, helping to develop, 82–83, 109–114, 129–131, 133–134
  as bright side of management, 165–167
  emotions of, understanding hidden, 105–109
  emphasizing enterprise, 131–132
  hurdles, 161–165
  learning from mistakes, 128–129
  listening effectively, 127–128
  obtaining information, 122–124
  powerful communications, 124–126
  promotion of, 135–136
  stereotypes, 169–171
  trouble makers, 172–173
  working with, principles of, 23–26, 86–87, 112–114, 118–119, 129–130, 133–134
Successes:
  of balanced person, 206
  of corporation person, 211–212
  equipping yourself for, 212–215
  of forgiving person, 210–211
  of involved individual, 207–208

Successes *(Cont.)*:
  of learner, 208–209
  of respectful person, 210
  of sense-of-humor person, 207
  of sensitive person, 209–210
  of uncrushables, 206–207

T

Tension, 38
Time:
  conscious of, 91
  manager of, 91
Traits, good character, 7
Troubles:
  handling, 83–84
  impersonal, 4
  people, 1, 173

U

Understanding impact of human interrelations, 2
United States:
  business, changes in, 66–67
  business population in, 46

V

Vision:
  mile, 158–161, 165
  short, 158–161, 165

W

Women's liberation, 163